MOVIES

The 80s were glory days for the Hollywood blockbuster, the cult classic and cinematic spoof. The Brat Pack reigned fist-in-the-air supreme as the nerd, the jock, the princess, the oddball, and the criminal all found a place to belong. Kids went on wild, goony adventures, and musclebound heroes spit scattered one-liners like machine-gun fire.

Are you a Top Gun of Trivia? Are you the Rain Man of 80s movie facts? Then gather your Heathers together, call up a Platoon of friends (or even just a bunch of Outsiders), and prove once and for all that, when it comes to 80s movie trivia, nobody puts you in a corner!

A LIFE OF CRIME
QUESTIONS

1 Change one letter in each of the words below to reveal the name of a 1985 drama, starring William Hurt as a prisoner in a Brazilian jail:

MISS IF SHE SLIDER ROMAN

2 For her role in which 1988 legal drama did Jodie Foster win the Academy Award for Best Actress?

3 Which two actors star in *Prizzi's Honor* as a pair of assassins hired to kill one another?

4 What is the title of the 1986 British crime drama, starring Bob Hoskins, which takes its name from a famous painting by Leonardo da Vinci?

5 Which actor, who had previously worked as a carpenter before finding worldwide fame, starred as a police sergeant in the 1985 drama, *Witness*?

6 In which 1983 film does Al Pacino play Tony Montana, a fictional mobster inspired by Al Capone?

7 For his role in which 1987 film, set in Prohibition-era Chicago, did Sean Connery win an Oscar for Best Actor in a Supporting Role?

A LIFE OF CRIME
ANSWERS

1 Change one letter in each of the words below to reveal the name of a 1985 drama, starring William Hurt as a prisoner in a Brazilian jail:

MISS IF SHE SLIDER ROMAN

Kiss of the Spider Woman

Set during the Brazilian military dictatorship, the film shows the interactions between Hurt's character and his cellmate, played by Raul Julia, for which role Hurt won the Academy Award for Best Actor. The film is an adaptation of the Spanish-language novel of the same name, published in 1976 and written by Manuel Puig.

2 For her role in which 1988 legal drama did Jodie Foster win the Academy Award for Best Actress?

The Accused

3 Which two actors star in *Prizzi's Honor* as a pair of assassins hired to kill one another?

Jack Nicholson and Kathleen Turner

4 What is the title of the 1986 British crime drama, starring Bob Hoskins, which takes its name from a famous painting by Leonardo da Vinci?

Mona Lisa

5 Which actor, who had previously worked as a carpenter before finding worldwide fame, starred as a police sergeant in the 1985 drama, *Witness*?

Harrison Ford

6 In which 1983 film does Al Pacino play Tony Montana, a fictional mobster inspired by Al Capone?

Scarface

7 For his role in which 1987 film, set in Prohibition-era Chicago, did Sean Connery win an Oscar for Best Actor in a Supporting Role?

The Untouchables

ACTION & ADVENTURE 1
QUESTIONS

1 How many *Indiana Jones* movies were released during the 1980s?

2 What is the name of the fictional Los Angeles building in which most of *Die Hard*'s action takes place?

3 Unjumble the letters below to reveal the name of *Scarface*'s director:

DAMNABLE PAIR (5, 2, 5)

4 In *The Princess Bride*, which character delivers an iconic line that ends with the words "You killed my father. Prepare to die"?

5 Which Oscar-winning actor —who later lent his name to prestigious UK stage awards —played the role of Zeus in 1981's *Clash of the Titans*?

6 *Take My Breath Away* won the Oscar for Best Original Song after appearing in which 1986 movie starring Tom Cruise?

7 What is the name of the legendary pirate whose treasure is hunted by the protagonists of Steven Spielberg's *The Goonies*?

ACTION & ADVENTURE 1
ANSWERS

1 How many *Indiana Jones* movies were released during the 1980s?

Three

The movies were Raiders of the Lost Ark *(1981),* Indiana Jones and the Temple of Doom *(1984), and* Indiana Jones and the Last Crusade *(1989). Although* The Temple of Doom *was the second release, it is actually a prequel to the first released movie, to which* The Last Crusade *is then a sequel. George Lucas had originally suggested the iconic action hero should have the name Indiana Smith, but the surname was changed by* Raiders of the Lost Ark *director Steven Spielberg.*

2 What is the name of the fictional Los Angeles building in which most of *Die Hard*'s action takes place?

Nakatomi Plaza

3 Unjumble the letters below to reveal the name of *Scarface*'s director:

DAMNABLE PAIR (5, 2, 5)

Brian de Palma

4 In *The Princess Bride*, which character delivers an iconic line that ends with the words "You killed my father. Prepare to die"?

Inigo Montoya, played by Mandy Patinkin

5 Which Oscar-winning actor—who later lent his name to prestigious UK stage awards—played the role of Zeus in 1981's *Clash of the Titans*?

Laurence Olivier

6 *Take My Breath Away* won the Oscar for Best Original Song after appearing in which 1986 movie starring Tom Cruise?

Top Gun

7 What is the name of the legendary pirate whose treasure is hunted by the protagonists of Steven Spielberg's *The Goonies*?

One-Eyed Willy

THE OSCARS: ACTORS
QUESTIONS

1 Who won the Oscar for Best Actor for his role as Christy Brown in *My Left Foot*?

2 Which actor won the Best Supporting Actor Oscar for his role in *An Officer and a Gentleman*?

3 For what starring role as the titular character in a 1982 biopic did Ben Kingsley win the Academy Award for Best Actor?

4 Which two actors were nominated for the Academy for Award for Best Supporting Actor for their roles in *Platoon*, although neither of them eventually won?

5 Fill in the gaps below to reveal the title of a 1981 film starring Henry Fonda and Katharine Hepburn, who both won Oscars for their roles:

O_ G_L_E_ P_N_

6 What is the title of the 1989 historical war drama for which Denzel Washington was awarded a Best Supporting Actor Oscar for his role?

7 What is the name of the character played by Paul Newman in *The Color of Money*, a role for which he won the Oscar for Best Actor?

THE OSCARS: ACTORS

ANSWERS

1 Who won the Oscar for Best Actor for his role as Christy Brown in *My Left Foot*?

Daniel Day-Lewis

> *The film was based on the real experiences of Christy Brown, a writer and painter with cerebral palsy who was only able to work with his left foot. Many of the scenes were filmed as mirror images, as Day-Lewis could only recreate Brown's dexterity using his own right foot.*

2 Which actor won the Best Supporting Actor Oscar for his role in *An Officer and a Gentleman*?

Louis Gossett Jr.

3 For what starring role as the titular character in a 1982 biopic did Ben Kingsley win the Academy Award for Best Actor?

Mahatma Gandhi

4 Which two actors were nominated for the Academy for Award for Best Supporting Actor for their roles in *Platoon*, although neither of them eventually won?

Willem Dafoe and Tom Berenger

5 Fill in the gaps below to reveal the title of a 1981 film starring Henry Fonda and Katharine Hepburn, who both won Oscars for their roles:

O_ G_L_E_ P_N_

On Golden Pond

6 What is the title of the 1989 historical war drama for which Denzel Washington was awarded a Best Supporting Actor Oscar for his role?

Glory

7 What is the name of the character played by Paul Newman in *The Color of Money*, a role for which he won the Oscar for Best Actor?

"Fast Eddie" Felson

BACK TO THE STAR WARS
QUESTIONS

1. What is the exact date that Marty McFly first travels back in time to, in *Back to the Future*?

2. On which planet does Luke Skywalker crash-land in *The Empire Strikes Back*, subsequently meeting Yoda for the first time?

3. What do the initials T.I.E. stand for in "TIE fighter", the fictional starships that appear throughout the *Star Wars* movies?

4. Who is Luke Skywalker's father, as revealed in the *Star Wars* sequel, *The Empire Strikes Back*?

5. In *Back to the Future II*, which footwear brand is depicted as having invented a pair of shoes with self-tying laces?

6. Change one letter in each word below to reveal the name of a song famously used on the soundtrack of *Back to the Future*, performed by Huey Lewis and the News:

   TIE POKER IF WOVE

7. Which character from the *Star Wars* movie series is currently frozen in carbonite on the planet Tatooine at the beginning of *Return of the Jedi*?

BACK TO THE STAR WARS
ANSWERS

1 What is the exact date that Marty McFly first travels back in time to, in *Back to the Future*?

November 5, 1955

> *The date of Marty McFly's arrival in the past reportedly changed several times after the screenplay had been initially written, as production for the film was pushed later and later. For the character to have traveled back in time exactly thirty years, the date had to be brought forward each time a year passed without the film being completed.*

2 On which planet does Luke Skywalker crash-land in *The Empire Strikes Back*, subsequently meeting Yoda for the first time?

Dagobah

3 What do the initials T.I.E. stand for in "TIE fighter", the fictional starships that appear throughout the *Star Wars* movies?

Twin Ion Engines

4 Who is Luke Skywalker's father, as revealed in the *Star Wars* sequel, *The Empire Strikes Back*?

Darth Vader

5 In *Back to the Future II*, which footwear brand is depicted as having invented a pair of shoes with self-tying laces?

Nike

6 Change one letter in each word below to reveal the name of a song famously used on the soundtrack of *Back to the Future*, performed by Huey Lewis and the News:

TIE POKER IF WOVE

The Power of Love

7 Which character from the *Star Wars* movie series is currently frozen in carbonite on the planet Tatooine at the beginning of *Return of the Jedi*?

Han Solo

BIOGRAPHICAL
QUESTIONS

1. Who directed the 1982 biopic *Gandhi*, winning the Academy Award for Best Director for his work?

2. What is the name of the hymn heard at the end of *Chariots of Fire*, whose lyrics inspired the film's title?

3. By what name is Joseph Merrick better known, which became the title of a 1980 biopic starring John Hurt?

4. What is the name of the Italian composer whose fictitious rivalry with Mozart is the focus of the 1984 period drama, *Amadeus*?

5. Change one letter in each word below to restore the name of a 1989 anti-war film, which stars Tom Cruise in the lead role:

   BURN OF TOE FOURTY
   IF DULY

6. Which boxer is played by Robert De Niro in *Raging Bull*, a film which is based on the sportsman's own memoir?

7. Who played the protagonist, Loretta Lynn, in *Coal Miner's Daughter*, a role for which she won the Oscar for Best Actress?

1 Who directed the 1982 biopic *Gandhi*, winning the Academy Award for Best Director for his work?

Richard Attenborough

The film also won the Best Picture Oscar, which Attenborough accepted in his role as the film's producer—Gandhi won eight Oscars overall. As an actor, Attenborough is perhaps best known to modern audiences for his role as the owner of the fictional Jurassic Park, in the original film directed by Steven Spielberg.

2 What is the name of the hymn heard at the end of *Chariots of Fire*, whose lyrics inspired the film's title?

Jerusalem

3 By what name is Joseph Merrick better known, which became the title of a 1980 biopic starring John Hurt?

The Elephant Man

4 What is the name of the Italian composer whose fictitious rivalry with Mozart is the focus of the 1984 period drama, *Amadeus*?

Antonio Salieri

5 Change one letter in each word below to restore the name of a 1989 anti-war film, which stars Tom Cruise in the lead role:

BURN OF TOE FOURTY IF DULY

Born on the Fourth of July

6 Which boxer is played by Robert De Niro in *Raging Bull*, a film which is based on the sportsman's own memoir?

Jake LaMotta

7 Who played the protagonist, Loretta Lynn, in *Coal Miner's Daughter*, a role for which she won the Oscar for Best Actress?

Sissy Spacek

COMEDY 1
QUESTIONS

1 Which 1981 film starring Dudley Moore and Liza Minnelli was nominated for an Academy Award for Best Screenplay Written Directly for the Screen?

2 Which 1980 musical comedy starred former *Saturday Night Live* members John Belushi and Dan Aykroyd as a pair of friends attempting to put their band back together?

3 Which British actress, who later went on to star in *Mamma Mia!* and the *Harry Potter* films, played the eponymous character in 1983's *Educating Rita*?

4 What is the name of the Buddy Holly song that lent its title to a 1986 film of the same name, starring Kathleen Turner in the titular role?

5 Rearrange the letters below to reveal the name of a 1980 film which served as a parody of earlier disaster movies:

REAL PAIN! (8)

6 Which actor starred in the 1982 romcom *Tootsie*, as out-of-work actor Michael Dorsey?

7 According to the 1988 film of the same name, how many times do you have to speak Beetlejuice's name before he can be summoned?

1 Which 1981 film starring Dudley Moore and Liza Minnelli was nominated for an Academy Award for Best Screenplay Written Directly for the Screen?

Arthur

The film was nominated for four Oscars in total, winning two: Best Original Song and Best Supporting Actor, for John Gielgud. Although the film's titular character had been written as an American, Dudley Moore's English accent is perhaps one of Arthur's most memorable characteristics.

2 Which 1980 musical comedy starred former *Saturday Night Live* members John Belushi and Dan Aykroyd as a pair of friends attempting to put their band back together?

The Blues Brothers

3 Which British actress, who later went on to star in *Mamma Mia!* and the *Harry Potter* films, played the eponymous character in 1983's *Educating Rita*?

Julie Walters

4 What is the name of the Buddy Holly song that lent its title to a 1986 film of the same name, starring Kathleen Turner in the titular role?

Peggy Sue Got Married

5 Rearrange the letters below to reveal the name of a 1980 film which served as a parody of earlier disaster movies:

REAL PAIN! (8)

Airplane!

6 Which actor starred in the 1982 romcom *Tootsie*, as out-of-work actor Michael Dorsey?

Dustin Hoffman

7 According to the 1988 film of the same name, how many times do you have to speak Beetlejuice's name before he can be summoned?

Three

E.T.
QUESTIONS

1 Composer John Williams included in his *E.T. the Extra-Terrestrial* score a musical reference to another space-related film which he had also composed the music for. Which one?

2 Which actor, who starred in the *Indiana Jones* film series, filmed a cameo as a school principal, which was not included in the final edit?

3 The role of Elliot's younger sister was the first major film appearance for which actress, who was seven years old when the film was released?

4 What is the name of the children's toy that features prominently in the machine built by E.T. in his attempt to "phone home"?

5 What kind of animals are shown being released into a classroom, to prevent them from being dissected in the school science lab?

6 In order to prevent the plot being leaked, the film was given which non-descript working title?
   a. *A Boy's Life*
   b. *Night Skies*
   c. *Growing Up*
   d. *Telephone Drama*

7 The young protagonist, Elliot, uses Reece's Pieces to lure E.T. out of his hiding place at the beginning of the film. Which three colors do the chocolate candy pieces come in?

1 Composer John Williams included in his *E.T. the Extra-Terrestrial* score a musical reference to another space-related film which he had also composed the music for. Which one?

Star Wars: Episode V—The Empire Strikes Back

> Yoda's Theme *is briefly hinted at in the* E.T. the Extra-Terrestrial *score, when E.T sees a child dressed as the* Star Wars *character Yoda, and appears to recognize the fellow alien character. The link is also acknowledged in the* Star Wars *film franchise, where a group of aliens similar to E.T. appear in* Star Wars: Episode I—The Phantom Menace.

2 Which actor, who starred in the *Indiana Jones* film series, filmed a cameo as a school principal, which was not included in the final edit?

Harrison Ford

3 The role of Elliot's younger sister was the first major film appearance for which actress, who was seven years old when the film was released?

Drew Barrymore

4 What is the name of the children's toy that features prominently in the machine built by E.T. in his attempt to "phone home"?

Speak & Spell

5 What kind of animals are shown being released into a classroom, to prevent them from being dissected in the school science lab?

Frogs

6 In order to prevent the plot being leaked, the film was given which non-descript working title?

a. *A Boy's Life*
b. *Night Skies*
c. *Growing Up*
d. *Telephone Drama*

a. *A Boy's Life*

7 The young protagonist, Elliot, uses Reece's Pieces to lure E.T. out of his hiding place at the beginning of the film. Which three colors do the chocolate candy pieces come in?

Orange, yellow, and brown

HORROR & THRILLER
QUESTIONS

1 What make and model of car is "Christine", in the 1983 film based on the novel of the same name by Steven King?

2 What is the name of the hotel in which much of the action in *The Shining* takes place?

3 In which English county is the protagonist first bitten in *An American Werewolf in London*?

4 What breed of dog is Cujo, in the 1983 horror film of the same name?

5 In which 1984 film did Robert Englund originate the character of Freddy Krueger?

6 Change one letter in each word below to reveal the name of a 1987 film starring Arnold Schwarzenegger in a dystopian future:

SHE CUNNING MAD

7 In *Deathtrap*, which British actor, known for often playing a Cockney, took the main role of Sidney Bruhl?

HORROR & THRILLER
ANSWERS

1 What make and model of car is "Christine", in the 1983 film based on the novel of the same name by Steven King?

Plymouth Fury

The iconic red and white car, which appears to have a mind of its own, was in fact played by a cast of several individual cars bought up by the film's director at the start of production. In real life, the car had only ever been produced in one color— a shade of white—so the paintwork described in the novel and shown in the film adaptation was a custom order.

2 What is the name of the hotel in which much of the action in *The Shining* takes place?

Overlook Hotel

3 In which English county is the protagonist first bitten in *An American Werewolf in London*?

North Yorkshire

4 What breed of dog is Cujo, in the 1983 horror film of the same name?

St Bernard

5 In which 1984 film did Robert Englund originate the character of Freddy Krueger?

A Nightmare on Elm Street

6 Change one letter in each word below to reveal the name of a 1987 film starring Arnold Schwarzenegger in a dystopian future:

SHE CUNNING MAD

The Running Man

7 In *Deathtrap*, which British actor, known for often playing a Cockney, took the main role of Sidney Bruhl?

Michael Caine

KIDS 1
QUESTIONS

1 Which number from *The Little Mermaid* won an Oscar for Best Original Song, beating another song from the same film?

2 What is the name of the character played by Carol Burnett in the 1982 musical *Annie*, who runs the orphanage in which Annie is living?

3 Which 1988 fantasy film created by Studio Ghibli has had every other letter removed from its title?

M_ _E_G_B_R _O_O_O

4 Which actor starred as Popeye in the 1980 film of the same name, opposite Shelley Duvall?

5 In which 1984 fantasy adventure film are the characters Urgl, Atreyu, and The Childlike Empress found?

6 Which 1989 stop-motion film starred the characters Wallace and Gromit on an adventure to the moon, as they attempted to find more cheese?

7 Change one letter in each word below to restore the name of a 1989 live-action Disney film starring Rick Moranis:

MONEY A SHRINK TOE BIDS

1 Which number from *The Little Mermaid* won an Oscar for Best Original Song, beating another song from the same film?

Under the Sea

Under the Sea and Kiss the Girl were both nominated for Best Original Song, and the film also won Best Original Score for the work of Alan Menken, the composer. With its calypso-inspired themes, and vocals from Samuel E. Wright, Under the Sea also won Menken and lyricist Howard Ashman a Grammy Award in 1991.

2 What is the name of the character played by Carol Burnett in the 1982 musical *Annie*, who runs the orphanage in which Annie is living?

Miss Agatha Hannigan

3 Which 1988 fantasy film created by Studio Ghibli has had every other letter removed from its title?

M_ _E_G_B_R _O_O_O

My Neighbor Totoro

4 Which actor starred as Popeye in the 1980 film of the same name, opposite Shelley Duvall?

Robin Williams

5 In which 1984 fantasy adventure film are the characters Urgl, Atreyu, and The Childlike Empress found?

The NeverEnding Story

6 Which 1989 stop-motion film starred the characters Wallace and Gromit on an adventure to the moon, as they attempted to find more cheese?

A Grand Day Out

7 Change one letter in each word below to restore the name of a 1989 live-action Disney film starring Rick Moranis:

MONEY A SHRINK TOE BIDS

Honey I Shrunk the Kids

TEENAGE KICKS 1
QUESTIONS

1. Which cult 1985 comedy drama opens with a description of its five protagonists as "a brain, an athlete, a basket case, a princess, and a criminal"?

2. What kind of contraption functions as the time machine used by the title characters in *Bill and Ted's Excellent Adventure*?

3. What is the name of the fortune-telling machine that grants the wishes of Josh Baskin, played by Tom Hanks, in *Big*?

4. In *Ferris Bueller's Day Off*, what is the make of car that Ferris borrows from his friend Cameron, which plunges into a ravine later in the film?

5. Which fantasy film, starring Michael J. Fox as a lycanthropic high schooler, was later adapted into a popular TV series of the same name?

6. Which song won the Academy Award for Best Original Song, after being used as the theme tune for the 1987 comedy drama *Dirty Dancing*?

7. What is the title of the 1983 dance-drama film which stars Jennifer Beals as a welder who hopes to become a professional dancer?

TEENAGE KICKS 1

ANSWERS

1 Which cult 1985 comedy drama opens with a description of its five protagonists as "a brain, an athlete, a basket case, a princess, and a criminal"?

The Breakfast Club

The film is one of the best-known coming-of-age pictures from the 1980s, whose cast came to be known as the "Brat Pack" after appearing together in several movies with similar themes. Two of the film's stars, Molly Ringwald and Anthony Michael Hall, had already appeared together the previous year, in Sixteen Candles.

2 What kind of contraption functions as the time machine used by the title characters in *Bill and Ted's Excellent Adventure*?

A telephone booth

3 What is the name of the fortune-telling machine that grants the wishes of Josh Baskin, played by Tom Hanks, in *Big*?

Zoltar

4 In *Ferris Bueller's Day Off*, what is the make of car that Ferris borrows from his friend Cameron, which plunges into a ravine later in the film?

Ferrari

5 Which fantasy film, starring Michael J. Fox as a lycanthropic high schooler, was later adapted into a popular TV series of the same name?

Teen Wolf

6 Which song won the Academy Award for Best Original Song, after being used as the theme tune for the 1987 comedy drama *Dirty Dancing*?

(I've Had) The Time of My Life

7 What is the title of the 1983 dance-drama film which stars Jennifer Beals as a welder who hopes to become a professional dancer?

Flashdance

THE OSCARS: ACTRESSES
QUESTIONS

1 Who won the Oscar for Best Actress in 1986 for her role in *Children of a Lesser God*, the first deaf actress to do so?

2 Which actress won a Best Supporting Actress Oscar for her role in *Prizzi's Honor*, a film which was directed by her father?

3 Who won the Oscar for Best Supporting Actress for her role in *Tootsie*, opposite Dustin Hoffman?

4 Change one letter in each word below to reveal the name of a 1984 film starring Sally Field, for which she won the Academy Award for Best Actress?

PLANES ON TOE HEARD

5 What is the name of the character played by Shirley MacLaine in the 1983 comedy drama, *Terms of Endearment*, for which she won the Best Actress Oscar?

6 Who became the first person to win an Oscar for portraying a character of the opposite sex, for her role in the film *The Year of Living Dangerously*?

7 For which 1989 comedy drama did Jessica Tandy win the Oscar for Best Actress after starring as the titular character, opposite Morgan Freeman?

THE OSCARS: ACTRESSES

ANSWERS

1 Who won the Oscar for Best Actress in 1986 for her role in *Children of a Lesser God*, the first deaf actress to do so?

Marlee Matlin

> *Playing a young, deaf janitor opposite William Hurt in his role as a hearing teacher, Matlin also became the youngest actress to win the Best Actress award, at age 21. Later, in 2021, Matlin took a supporting role in* CODA, *which went on to win Best Picture at the Oscars.*

2 Which actress won a Best Supporting Actress Oscar for her role in *Prizzi's Honor*, a film which was directed by her father?

Anjelica Huston

3 Who won the Oscar for Best Supporting Actress for her role in *Tootsie*, opposite Dustin Hoffman?

Jessica Lange

4 Change one letter in each word below to reveal the name of a 1984 film starring Sally Field, for which she won the Academy Award for Best Actress?

PLANES ON TOE HEARD

Places in the Heart

5 What is the name of the character played by Shirley MacLaine in the 1983 comedy drama, *Terms of Endearment*, for which she won the Best Actress Oscar?

Aurora Greenway

6 Who became the first person to win an Oscar for portraying a character of the opposite sex, for her role in the film *The Year of Living Dangerously*?

Linda Hunt

7 For which 1989 comedy drama did Jessica Tandy win the Oscar for Best Actress after starring as the titular character, opposite Morgan Freeman?

Driving Miss Daisy

POT LUCK 1
QUESTIONS

1. With which 1987 psychological thriller, starring Glenn Close, is the expression "bunny boiler" best associated?

2. What is the name of the titular character's toon wife in *Who Framed Roger Rabbit*?

3. Which real-life brothers starred opposite Michelle Pfeiffer in the 1989 musical drama, *The Fabulous Baker Boys*?

4. Which 1985 film, starring Whoopi Goldberg and directed by Steven Spielberg, is an adaptation of a novel of the same name written by Alice Walker?

5. What is the name of the main character in *The Land Before Time*, a young apatosaurus dinosaur who loses his mother in the film's opening scenes?

6. Who wrote, produced, and directed, as well as starred in, both 1986's *She's Gotta Have It* and 1989's *Do the Right Thing*?

7. Delete one letter from each pair below to reveal the title of a 1988 romantic comedy starring Tom Cruise:

   CT OP CO KP TG UA NI LN

1 With which 1987 psychological thriller, starring Glenn Close, is the expression "bunny boiler" best associated?

Fatal Attraction

Close was nominated for an Oscar for her role as the spurned lover of a married man, played by Michael Douglas. In perhaps the film's most famous scene, Close's character boils the pet rabbit of her lover's child on the family stove, giving life to the expression "bunny boiler" as a way of describing a disturbingly obsessive person.

2 What is the name of the titular character's toon wife in *Who Framed Roger Rabbit*?

Jessica Rabbit

3 Which real-life brothers starred opposite Michelle Pfeiffer in the 1989 musical drama, *The Fabulous Baker Boys*?

Jeff and Beau Bridges

4 Which 1985 film, starring Whoopi Goldberg and directed by Steven Spielberg, is an adaptation of a novel of the same name written by Alice Walker?

The Color Purple

5 What is the name of the main character in *The Land Before Time*, a young apatosaurus dinosaur who loses his mother in the film's opening scenes?

Littlefoot

6 Who wrote, produced, and directed, as well as starred in, both 1986's *She's Gotta Have It* and 1989's *Do the Right Thing*?

Spike Lee

7 Delete one letter from each pair below to reveal the title of a 1988 romantic comedy starring Tom Cruise:

CT OP CO KP TG UA NI LN

Cocktail

SCI-FI
QUESTIONS

1. In which 1986 sequel, directed by James Cameron, did Sigourney Weaver reprise her role as Ellen Ripley?

2. Which rock band composed most of the soundtrack for the 1984 space epic, *Dune*, which followed on from the success of their 1982 hit song, *Africa*?

3. Which 1982 film, directed by Ridley Scott, is an adaptation of a Philip K. Dick novel entitled *Do Androids Dream of Electric Sheep*?

4. *RoboCop* is set in a futuristic version of which Michigan city?

5. In which specific building is the first paranormal activity seen, at the beginning of *Ghostbusters*?

6. Rearrange the letters below to reveal the name of a 1982 film by Terry Gilliam, starring two of his fellow Monty Python members:

   BITTEN MAIDS (4, 7)

7. Which 1980 film, based on a comic strip of the same name, starred Sam J. Jones as a football player battling against the extraterrestrial dictator Ming the Merciless?

SCI-FI
ANSWERS

1 In which 1986 sequel, directed by James Cameron, did Sigourney Weaver reprise her role as Ellen Ripley?

Aliens

> *A sequel to the 1979 classic* Alien, Aliens *created a fresh challenge for the pioneering character of Ripley, who had been frozen in time since the events of the previous film. Weaver was nominated for the Academy Award for Best Actress for the role, although she ultimately lost.*

2 Which rock band composed most of the soundtrack for the 1984 space epic, *Dune*, which followed on from the success of their 1982 hit song, *Africa*?

Toto

3 Which 1982 film, directed by Ridley Scott, is an adaptation of a Philip K. Dick novel entitled *Do Androids Dream of Electric Sheep*?

Blade Runner

4 *RoboCop* is set in a futuristic version of which Michigan city?

Detroit

5 In which specific building is the first paranormal activity seen, at the beginning of *Ghostbusters*?

New York Public Library

6 Rearrange the letters below to reveal the name of a 1982 film by Terry Gilliam, starring two of his fellow Monty Python members:

BITTEN MAIDS (4, 7)

Time Bandits

7 Which 1980 film, based on a comic strip of the same name, starred Sam J. Jones as a football player battling against the extraterrestrial dictator Ming the Merciless?

Flash Gordon

SIGOURNEY WEAVER
QUESTIONS

1. Which Australian actor starred opposite Weaver in the 1982 romantic drama, *The Year of Living Dangerously*, set in Indonesia?

2. What is the profession of Weaver's character, Dana, in *Ghostbusters*?

3. Which film, set primarily in Rwanda, starred Weaver as real-life naturalist Dian Fossey?

4. Change one letter in each word below to reveal the name of a 1986 thriller starring Weaver and Michael Caine, whose name is taken from a London road:

   HALT MOOR STREEL

5. What is the name of the character played by Weaver in *Working Girl*, who steals the ideas of her secretary, played by Melanie Griffith?

6. Which actor, famous for his role in *The Sound of Music*, starred with Weaver and William Hurt in the 1981 mystery *Eyewitness*?

7. For which 1986 film did Weaver earn an Academy Award nomination for Best Actress, the first such nomination for a science fiction film?

SIGOURNEY WEAVER

ANSWERS

1 Which Australian actor starred opposite Weaver in the 1982 romantic drama, *The Year of Living Dangerously*, set in Indonesia?

Mel Gibson

> *Gibson played a foreign correspondent attempting to report on the political situation in Jakarta, with Weaver playing a British Embassy attaché. Gibson, as well as other members of the production team, received death threats for the film, which was banned in Indonesia.*

2 What is the profession of Weaver's character, Dana, in *Ghostbusters*?

Musician

3 Which film, set primarily in Rwanda, starred Weaver as real-life naturalist Dian Fossey?

Gorillas in the Mist

4 Change one letter in each word below to reveal the name of a 1986 thriller starring Weaver and Michael Caine, whose name is taken from a London road:

HALT MOOR STREEL

Half Moon Street

5 What is the name of the character played by Weaver in *Working Girl*, who steals the ideas of her secretary, played by Melanie Griffith?

Katharine Parker

6 Which actor, famous for his role in *The Sound of Music*, starred with Weaver and William Hurt in the 1981 mystery *Eyewitness*?

Christopher Plummer

7 For which 1986 film did Weaver earn an Academy Award nomination for Best Actress, the first such nomination for a science fiction film?

Aliens

COMEDY 2
QUESTIONS

1. Which actor and singer won the Oscar for Best Actress for her role in the 1987 romcom, *Moonstruck*?

2. In which 1989 adventure comedy do Keanu Reeves and Alex Winter play a pair of high schoolers who travel through time to alter history?

3. What is the title of the 1984 mockumentary film that focuses on a fictional British rock band named after a piece of medical equipment?

4. In which 1989 film, written by Nora Ephron, does the line "I'll have what she's having" famously feature in a restaurant scene?

5. In which luxurious New York seaside resort does most of the action in the 1989 comedy *Weekend at Bernie's* take place?

6. What is the make of the car owned by the parents of Tom Cruise's character in *Risky Business*, which sinks into Lake Michigan during the film?

7. Rearrange the letters below to reveal the title of a 1983 comedy set in Scotland, in which an oil company attempts to buy an entire town:

   COAL OR HEL (5, 4)

COMEDY 2
ANSWERS

1 Which actor and singer won the Oscar for Best Actress for her role in the 1987 romcom, *Moonstruck*?

Cher

Cher stars as Loretta Castorini, an Italian-American widow who falls in love with her fiancé's younger brother, played by Nicolas Cage. Cher had previously been nominated at the Academy Awards for Best Supporting Actress for her role in the 1984 drama Silkwood, opposite Meryl Streep.

2 In which 1989 adventure comedy do Keanu Reeves and Alex Winter play a pair of high schoolers who travel through time to alter history?

Bill & Ted's Excellent Adventure

3 What is the title of the 1984 mockumentary film that focuses on a fictional British rock band named after a piece of medical equipment?

This Is Spinal Tap

4 In which 1989 film, written by Nora Ephron, does the line "I'll have what she's having" famously feature in a restaurant scene?

When Harry Met Sally

5 In which luxurious New York seaside resort does most of the action in the 1989 comedy *Weekend at Bernie's* take place?

The Hamptons

6 What is the make of the car owned by the parents of Tom Cruise's character in *Risky Business*, which sinks into Lake Michigan during the film?

Porsche

7 Rearrange the letters below to reveal the title of a 1983 comedy set in Scotland, in which an oil company attempts to buy an entire town:

COAL OR HEL (5, 4)

Local Hero

MILITARY
QUESTIONS

1 Who starred as the radio DJ sent in to shake up the broadcasts and boost military morale in *Good Morning, Vietnam*?

2 Delete one letter in each pair below to reveal the name of a 1981 comedy in which Bill Murray's character enlists in the US Army:

NS AT IR IO NP AE LS

3 Which romantic film, starring Richard Gere, takes its title from a military phrase used to describe how those in authority must be respectable?

4 Which West German film released in 1981, set aboard a U-boat during World War II, received six Academy Award nominations?

5 Who directed *Full Metal Jacket*, seven years after the success of their 1980 thriller *The Shining*?

6 What is the title of the 1986 film, starring Charlie Sheen, in which the protagonist struggles with the infighting of two of his superior officers during the Vietnam War?

7 Rearrange the letters below to reveal the title of a 1987 film, directed by Steven Spielberg and starring Christian Bale:

NO SUPREME THIEF
(6, 2, 3, 3)

1 Who starred as the radio DJ sent in to shake up the broadcasts and boost military morale in *Good Morning, Vietnam*?

Robin Williams

Williams's character was inspired by real-life radio DJ Adrian Cronauer, whose catchphrase gives the movie its name. The two did not meet during production on the express wishes of the film's director, to avoid too many similarities between the man and the character. Williams was nominated for an Academy Award for Best Actor for the role.

2 Delete one letter in each pair below to reveal the name of a 1981 comedy in which Bill Murray's character enlists in the US Army:

NS AT IR IO NP AE LS

Stripes

3 Which romantic film, starring Richard Gere, takes its title from a military phrase used to describe how those in authority must be respectable?

An Officer and a Gentleman

4 Which West German film released in 1981, set aboard a U-boat during World War II, received six Academy Award nominations?

Das Boot

5 Who directed *Full Metal Jacket*, seven years after the success of their 1980 thriller *The Shining*?

Stanley Kubrick

6 What is the title of the 1986 film, starring Charlie Sheen, in which the protagonist struggles with the infighting of two of his superior officers during the Vietnam War?

Platoon

7 Rearrange the letters below to reveal the title of a 1987 film, directed by Steven Spielberg and starring Christian Bale:

NO SUPREME THIEF (6, 2, 3, 3)

Empire of the Sun

ACTION & ADVENTURE 2
QUESTIONS

1 Which actor, who later went on to star as Jenny in *Forrest Gump*, played the eponymous Princess in *The Princess Bride*?

2 Change one letter in each word below to reveal the name of a song by The Righteous Brothers which appears in *Top Gun*:

YOU'SE LOUT WHAT MOVIN' FEEDIN'

3 Which 1981 fantasy film, named after a mythical sword, stars Helen Mirren, Liam Neeson, and Patrick Stewart as characters from Arthurian legend?

4 Who played Conan the Barbarian in the 1982 sword and sorcery epic of the same name?

5 In which 1984 martial arts film does the expression "sweep the leg" feature as an instruction to win by any means?

6 In which 1986 fantasy adventure does David Bowie star as Jareth, the Goblin King?

7 Which actor played Indiana Jones's father in *Indiana Jones and the Last Crusade*?

1 Which actor, who later went on to star as Jenny in *Forrest Gump*, played the eponymous Princess in *The Princess Bride*?

Robin Wright

Seven years before her starring role in Forrest Gump, *Robin Wright charmed audiences as the titular Princess Buttercup in the 1987 comedy-fantasy classic. The film is an adaptation of the screenwriter William Goldman's novel of the same name. He also wrote* Butch Cassidy and the Sundance Kid *and* All the President's Men.

2 Change one letter in each word below to reveal the name of a song by The Righteous Brothers which appears in *Top Gun*:

YOU'SE LOUT WHAT MOVIN' FEEDIN'

You've Lost That Lovin' Feelin'

3 Which 1981 fantasy film, named after a mythical sword, stars Helen Mirren, Liam Neeson, and Patrick Stewart as characters from Arthurian legend?

Excalibur

4 Who played Conan the Barbarian in the 1982 sword and sorcery epic of the same name?

Arnold Schwarzenegger

5 In which 1984 martial arts film does the expression "sweep the leg" feature as an instruction to win by any means?

The Karate Kid

6 In which 1986 fantasy adventure does David Bowie star as Jareth, the Goblin King?

Labyrinth

7 Which actor played Indiana Jones's father in *Indiana Jones and the Last Crusade*?

Sean Connery

POT LUCK 2
QUESTIONS

1 Which 1982 film, directed by Steven Spielberg, was the top-grossing film of the decade?

2 *Beverly Hills Cop* and *Coming to America* both starred which former *Saturday Night Live* cast member?

3 Which comedian and actor was nominated for an Academy Award for Best Actor for his lead role in the 1989 film, *Dead Poets Society*?

4 What is the name of the central protagonist in *Die Hard*?

5 The 1989 film, *Batman*, starred Val Kilmer as Batman. True or false?

6 Restore the missing vowels and change the spaces to reveal which two of its principal cast wrote the script for the 1984 supernatural comedy, *Ghostbusters*:

D NY KR YD and HRL DR M S

7 When Marty returns to Twin Pines Mall towards the end of the 1985 film, *Back to the Future*, the name of the mall has changed. What to, and why?

POT LUCK 2
ANSWERS

1 Which 1982 film, directed by Steven Spielberg, was the top-grossing film of the decade?

E.T. the Extra-Terrestrial

The iconic titular character was based on an imaginary friend that Spielberg had created for himself as a child, although its facial features in the film were modelled on the very real Carl Sandburg, Albert Einstein and Ernest Hemingway. The movie remained the highest-grossing film of all time for over a decade, until it was replaced by another Spielberg film in 1993: Jurassic Park.

2 *Beverly Hills Cop* and *Coming to America* both starred which former *Saturday Night Live* cast member?

Eddie Murphy

3 Which comedian and actor was nominated for an Academy Award for Best Actor for his lead role in the 1989 film, *Dead Poets Society*?

Robin Williams

4 What is the name of the central protagonist in *Die Hard*?

John McClane

5 The 1989 film, *Batman*, starred Val Kilmer as Batman. True or false?

False—it was Michael Keaton

6 Restore the missing vowels and change the spaces to reveal which two of its principal cast wrote the script for the 1984 supernatural comedy, *Ghostbusters*:

D NY KR YD and HRL DR M S

Dan Aykroyd and Harold Ramis

7 When Marty returns to Twin Pines Mall towards the end of the 1985 film, *Back to the Future*, the name of the mall has changed. What to, and why?

Lone Pine Mall, since when he journeyed back to 1955 he accidentally destroyed one of the immature pine trees

THE OSCARS
QUESTIONS

1. Which actor won the Oscar for Best Director in his directorial debut, seven years after being nominated for a Best Actor award for his role in *The Sting*?

2. Fill in the gaps below, with one letter per gap, to reveal the name of a 1988 drama in which Geena Davis starred, for which she won the Oscar for Best Supporting Actress:

   T_E A_C_D_N_A_
   T_U_I_T

3. Which musician won the Oscar for Best Original Song Score for his work on a 1984 rock musical which shares its name with his sixth studio album?

4. Who directed the 1989 deep-sea drama *The Abyss*, which won the Oscar for Best Visual Effects, much of which was shot underwater?

5. Which song by Stevie Wonder won the Oscar for Best Original Song after its appearance in the 1984 comedy, *The Woman in Red*?

6. Which 1988 supernatural comedy film, starring Michael Keaton as the title character, won the Academy Award for Best Makeup?

7. For which 1982 film was the winner of Best Original Song, *Up Where We Belong*, written?

THE OSCARS
ANSWERS

1 Which actor won the Oscar for Best Director in his directorial debut, seven years after being nominated for a Best Actor award for his role in *The Sting*?

Robert Redford

The film starred Donald Sutherland and Mary Tyler Moore, marking a departure for Moore from her usual light-hearted and comedic roles. She was nominated for Best Actress at the Academy Awards, and the film also won Best Picture. It had an overall total of six Oscar nominations.

2 Fill in the gaps below, with one letter per gap, to reveal the name of a 1988 drama in which Geena Davis starred, for which she won the Oscar for Best Supporting Actress:

T_E A_C_D_N_A_ T_U_I_T

The Accidental Tourist

3 Which musician won the Oscar for Best Original Song Score for his work on a 1984 rock musical which shares its name with his sixth studio album?

Prince—for *Purple Rain*

4 Who directed the 1989 deep-sea drama *The Abyss*, which won the Oscar for Best Visual Effects, much of which was shot underwater?

James Cameron

5 Which song by Stevie Wonder won the Oscar for Best Original Song after its appearance in the 1984 comedy, *The Woman in Red*?

I Just Called to Say I Love You

6 Which 1988 supernatural comedy film, starring Michael Keaton as the title character, won the Academy Award for Best Makeup?

Beetlejuice

7 For which 1982 film was the winner of Best Original Song, *Up Where We Belong*, written?

An Officer and a Gentleman

MOVIE MUSICALS
QUESTIONS

1 Which actress starred as the titular character in the 1983 romantic musical drama *Yentl*, which she also directed?

2 Which puppeteer, best known for his work with the Muppets, directed 1986's *Labyrinth*?

3 In *Little Shop of Horrors*, what does the film's protagonist, played by Rick Moranis, name the flesh-eating alien plant?

4 What is the name of the 1982 comedy musical, set in Paris, in which Julie Andrews plays a character pretending to be a man acting as a female impersonator?

5 Which 1988 comedy, starring Rikki Lake and Debbie Harry, was later turned into a Broadway musical of the same name, and then later still a musical film starring Zac Efron?

6 Change one letter in each word below to reveal the name of a 1988 science fiction musical, starring Jeff Goldblum and Geena Davis?

GARTH GILLS ACE EAST

7 Which 1980 musical, set in a New York performing arts school, features a title song that won the Oscar for Best Original Song?

MOVIE MUSICALS
ANSWERS

1 Which actress starred as the titular character in the 1983 romantic musical drama *Yentl*, which she also directed?

Barbra Streisand

Two of the film's songs, performed by Streisand, were nominated for Best Original Song at the Oscars, although neither of them won. Streisand won the Golden Globe for Best Director for her work, the first woman to win the award.

2 Which puppeteer, best known for his work with the Muppets, directed 1986's *Labyrinth*?

Jim Henson

3 In *Little Shop of Horrors*, what does the film's protagonist, played by Rick Moranis, name the flesh-eating alien plant?

Audrey II

4 What is the name of the 1982 comedy musical, set in Paris, in which Julie Andrews plays a character pretending to be a man acting as a female impersonator?

Victor/Victoria

5 Which 1988 comedy, starring Rikki Lake and Debbie Harry, was later turned into a Broadway musical of the same name, and then later still a musical film starring Zac Efron?

Hairspray

6 Change one letter in each word below to reveal the name of a 1988 science fiction musical, starring Jeff Goldblum and Geena Davis?

GARTH GILLS ACE EAST

Earth Girls Are Easy

7 Which 1980 musical, set in a New York performing arts school, features a title song that won the Oscar for Best Original Song?

Fame

MERYL STREEP
QUESTIONS

1. Change one letter in each word below to reveal the title of a 1982 film starring Meryl Streep, which borrows visual themes from several Hitchcock movies:

SKILL IF SHE FIGHT

2. Which 1986 comedy starring Streep and Jack Nicholson was an adaptation of a Nora Ephron novel of the same name?

3. Who starred opposite Streep, in the 1985 epic drama *Out of Africa*, as the English aristocrat Denys Finch Hatton?

4. In which country is the film *Evil Angels*, released in some territories as *A Cry in the Dark*, set? It tells the real-life story of the disappearance of a baby from an isolated campsite.

5. What is the title of the 1984 romcom starring Streep and Robert De Niro as a couple who meet on Christmas Eve in a bookstore, and accidentally mix up their gifts?

6. For her role in which 1981 film, starring Jeremy Irons, did Streep earn her first Academy Award nomination for Best Actress in a Leading Role?

7. What is the nationality of the eponymous character played by Streep in the 1982 drama *Sophie's Choice*, a role for which she won an Oscar for Best Actress?

MERYL STREEP
ANSWERS

1 Change one letter in each word below to reveal the title of a 1982 film starring Meryl Streep, which borrows visual themes from several Hitchcock movies:

SKILL IF SHE FIGHT

Still of the Night

Scenes from Vertigo *and* Rear Window, *as well as those from other Hitchcock films, are said to have inspired sequences in* Still of the Night. *Jessica Tandy, who starred in the 1982 movie as the mother of Streep's love interest, also previously appeared in the Hitchcock classic* The Birds.

2 Which 1986 comedy starring Streep and Jack Nicholson was an adaptation of a Nora Ephron novel of the same name?

Heartburn

3 Who starred opposite Streep, in the 1985 epic drama *Out of Africa*, as the English aristocrat Denys Finch Hatton?

Robert Redford

4 In which country is the film *Evil Angels*, released in some territories as *A Cry in the Dark*, set? It tells the real-life story of the disappearance of a baby from an isolated campsite.

Australia

5 What is the title of the 1984 romcom starring Streep and Robert De Niro as a couple who meet on Christmas Eve in a bookstore, and accidentally mix up their gifts?

Falling in Love

6 For her role in which 1981 film, starring Jeremy Irons, did Streep earn her first Academy Award nomination for Best Actress in a Leading Role?

The French Lieutenant's Woman

7 What is the nationality of the eponymous character played by Streep in the 1982 drama *Sophie's Choice*, a role for which she won an Oscar for Best Actress?

Polish

TEENAGE KICKS 2
QUESTIONS

1 How many of the lead characters in the 1989 black comedy *Heathers* have the name Heather?

2 Which 1984 film stars Molly Ringwald as a high schooler whose parents appear to have completely forgotten her birthday?

3 What is the title of the song by Cyndi Lauper which inspired a 1985 film of the same name, starring Sarah Jessica Parker and Helen Hunt?

4 In *Risky Business*, which US university does the protagonist's father wish him to attend?

5 Which actor starred as the central protagonist, Ren, in the 1984 musical drama *Footloose*?

6 Change one letter in each word below to reveal the name of a 1987 film, starring Patrick Dempsey, which takes its title from a song by The Beatles:

CAP'T BUT MY LIVE

7 Who directed 1983 drama *The Outsiders*, which features an ensemble cast that includes Tom Cruise, Emilio Estevez, Patrick Swayze, and Rob Lowe?

1 How many of the lead characters in the 1989 black comedy *Heathers* have the name Heather?

Three

Heather Duke, Heather Chandler, and Heather McNamara are three eponymous characters who star opposite Winona Ryder's character Veronica as the members of an exclusive high-school clique. The cult macabre comedy was adapted into an off-Broadway musical that later transferred to London's West End.

2 Which 1984 film stars Molly Ringwald as a high schooler whose parents appear to have completely forgotten her birthday?

Sixteen Candles

3 What is the title of the song by Cyndi Lauper which inspired a 1985 film of the same name, starring Sarah Jessica Parker and Helen Hunt?

Girls Just Want to Have Fun

4 In *Risky Business*, which US university does the protagonist's father wish him to attend?

Princeton University

5 Which actor starred as the central protagonist, Ren, in the 1984 musical drama *Footloose*?

Kevin Bacon

6 Change one letter in each word below to reveal the name of a 1987 film, starring Patrick Dempsey, which takes its title from a song by The Beatles:

CAP'T BUT MY LIVE

Can't Buy Me Love

7 Who directed 1983 drama *The Outsiders*, which features an ensemble cast that includes Tom Cruise, Emilio Estevez, Patrick Swayze, and Rob Lowe?

Francis Ford Coppola

COMEDY 3
QUESTIONS

1 In *Beverly Hills Cop*, what piece of fruit does Axel Foley use to incapacitate the car of the two police officers who are following him?

2 In which 1984 adventure comedy, starring Michael Douglas and Kathleen Turner, do the protagonists travel to Colombia in search of an emerald nicknamed "El Corazón"?

3 Can you change one letter in each word below to reveal the Carly Simon track which plays in the opening credits for *Working Girl*, and which won an Oscar for Best Original Song?

LIT SHE RAVER GUN

4 Which film about a trio of young waitresses, starring Julia Roberts and Annabeth Gish, is named after the fictional restaurant in which they all work?

5 What is the title of the 1987 film starring Goldie Hawn as an heiress who loses her memory after falling off a yacht?

6 Which Academy-Award-winning actor starred opposite Daryl Hannah in the 1984 fantasy romcom, *Splash*?

7 Which actor famous for his role in *Grease* starred opposite Kirstie Alley in the 1989 romcom, *Look Who's Talking*?

COMEDY 3
ANSWERS

1 In *Beverly Hills Cop*, what piece of fruit does Axel Foley use to incapacitate the car of the two police officers who are following him?

A banana

> In the famous "banana in the tailpipe" scene, Eddie Murphy's character sends down food to distract the officers while he sabotages their pursuit car. Murphy had starred opposite his fellow Saturday Night Live cast member Dan Aykroyd in Trading Places in the previous year, but it was Beverly Hills Cop that cemented his status as an international star.

2 In which 1984 adventure comedy, starring Michael Douglas and Kathleen Turner, do the protagonists travel to Colombia in search of an emerald nicknamed "El Corazón"?

Romancing the Stone

3 Can you change one letter in each word below to reveal the Carly Simon track which plays in the opening credits for *Working Girl*, and which won an Oscar for Best Original Song?

LIT SHE RAVER GUN

Let the River Run

4 Which film about a trio of young waitresses, starring Julia Roberts and Annabeth Gish, is named after the fictional restaurant in which they all work?

Mystic Pizza

5 What is the title of the 1987 film starring Goldie Hawn as an heiress who loses her memory after falling off a yacht?

Overboard

6 Which Academy-Award-winning actor starred opposite Daryl Hannah in the 1984 fantasy romcom, *Splash*?

Tom Hanks

7 Which actor famous for his role in *Grease* starred opposite Kirstie Alley in the 1989 romcom, *Look Who's Talking*?

John Travolta

DRAMA
QUESTIONS

1 Which sports drama, starring Ben Cross and Ian Charleson as Olympic athletes, won the Oscar for Best Picture in 1981?

2 For which 1984 biographical drama were Tom Hulce and F. Murray Abraham both nominated for a Best Actor in a Leading Role Oscar, which Abraham won?

3 Change one letter in each word below to reveal the name of a 1985 film starring Maggie Smith, adapted from a novel of the same name:

I ROAM WISH I VIED

4 In which country is the 1988 period drama *Dangerous Liaisons* set, starring Glenn Close and John Malkovich?

5 What is the title of the 1984 crime drama, starring Robert de Niro, which was released in Europe with a running time of 229 minutes?

6 Which actor won an Oscar for his leading role in the 1988 comedy drama *Rain Man*, opposite Tom Cruise?

7 Which poem by Walt Whitman is famously recited in the final scenes of *Dead Poets Society*?

1 Which sports drama, starring Ben Cross and Ian Charleson as Olympic athletes, won the Oscar for Best Picture in 1981?

Chariots of Fire

> *The biographical drama depicted the trials of two real athletes, Eric Liddell and Harold Abrahams, who competed in the 1924 Olympics. A third athlete, Douglas Lowe, was originally written into the script as a third protagonist, but he declined to be involved. The famous running scene was shot in St. Andrews, Scotland.*

2 For which 1984 biographical drama were Tom Hulce and F. Murray Abraham both nominated for a Best Actor in a Leading Role Oscar, which Abraham won?

Amadeus

3 Change one letter in each word below to reveal the name of a 1985 film starring Maggie Smith, adapted from a novel of the same name:

I ROAM WISH I VIED

A Room with a View

4 In which country is the 1988 period drama *Dangerous Liaisons* set, starring Glenn Close and John Malkovich?

France

5 What is the title of the 1984 crime drama, starring Robert de Niro, which was released in Europe with a running time of 229 minutes?

Once Upon a Time in America

6 Which actor won an Oscar for his leading role in the 1988 comedy drama *Rain Man*, opposite Tom Cruise?

Dustin Hoffman

7 Which poem by Walt Whitman is famously recited in the final scenes of *Dead Poets Society*?

O Captain! My Captain!

POT LUCK 3
QUESTIONS

1 Which lawn sport is shown being played by the principal characters in the opening scenes of *Heathers*?

2 In which mobster movie does the famous line "Say hello to my little friend" appear?

3 In *When Harry Met Sally*, who played the role of Sally's friend, Marie?

4 Which 1980 comedy, starring Jane Fonda, Dolly Parton, and Lily Tomlin, features a theme song of the same name written and performed by Parton?

5 Which actor played the named character in the title of the 1987 comedy drama *Withnail and I*?

6 What is the name of Ariel's love interest in the Disney-animated movie, *The Little Mermaid*?

7 Restore the missing vowels to reveal the name of a 1984 gangster film:

NC PN TM N MRC

8 Which 1986 movie centers on a robot known as Number 5?

9 Why were the scenes from the end of *Back to the Future* reshot for use at the start of *Back to the Future Part II*?

1 Which lawn sport is shown being played by the principal characters in the opening scenes of *Heathers*?

Croquet

> *A particular rule in croquet—which allows players to ruin another player's game by casting their ball out of the field of play—is shown in the film's opening scenes, foreshadowing the cut-throat nature of the high-school clique.*

2 In which mobster movie does the famous line "Say hello to my little friend" appear?

Scarface

3 In *When Harry Met Sally*, who played the role of Sally's friend, Marie?

Carrie Fisher

4 Which 1980 comedy, starring Jane Fonda, Dolly Parton, and Lily Tomlin, features a theme song of the same name written and performed by Parton?

9 to 5

5 Which actor played the named character in the title of the 1987 comedy drama *Withnail and I*?

Richard E. Grant

6 What is the name of Ariel's love interest in the Disney-animated movie, *The Little Mermaid*?

Prince Eric

7 Restore the missing vowels to reveal the name of a 1984 gangster film:

NC PN TM N MRC

Once Upon a Time in America

8 Which 1986 movie centers on a robot known as Number 5?

Short Circuit

9 Why were the scenes from the end of *Back to the Future* reshot for use at the start of *Back to the Future Part II*?

The role of Marty's girlfriend, Jennifer, had been recast

TV SHOWS

The 80s were The Wonder Years of transformation in television, where networks and creators started pushing the boundaries of content and genre. It saw the rise of the super-smooth TV detective drama, the prime-time soap opera and the family-based sitcom. And, by the power of Greyskull, it was a massive era for animated TV.

Do you pity the fool who would take you on in 80s TV trivia? Then call up your A-Team, and your Golden Girls (or even a bunch of Perfect Strangers) until you've got a Full House, and Quantum Leap your way through this round. Cowabunga, dude!

US COMEDY
QUESTIONS

1. The head bartender in *Cheers*, Sam Malone, was the former relief pitcher for which baseball team?

2. What were the names of Al and Peggy's kids in *Married... With Children*?

3. In which year did the final season of *M*A*S*H* air?

4. Rearrange the following letters to reveal the original last name of John Stamos's character in *Full House*:

   ARCH CON (7)

5. As well as being American, Betty White's character in *The Golden Girls* shares ancestral roots with which European country?

6. How many consecutive Emmy Awards did Michael J. Fox win for his role on *Family Ties*?

7. Restore the missing vowels to reveal the name of the street on which the Conners lived in the show *Roseanne*:

   DLWR

1 The head bartender in *Cheers*, Sam Malone, was the former relief pitcher for which baseball team?

Boston Red Sox

> *Portrayed by actor Ted Danson, Sam(uel) Malone's nickname on the team was "Mayday Malone". He left high school early in order to play professional baseball, with a major league career lasting about five years. He trades on this fading fame throughout the eleven seasons of the show.*

2 What were the names of Al and Peggy's kids in *Married... With Children*?

Bud and Kelly

3 In which year did the final season of *M*A*S*H* air?

1982

4 Rearrange the following letters to reveal the original last name of John Stamos's character in *Full House*:

ARCH CON (7)

Cochran

5 As well as being American, Betty White's character in *The Golden Girls* shares ancestral roots with which European country?

Norway

6 How many consecutive Emmy Awards did Michael J. Fox win for his role on *Family Ties*?

Three

7 Restore the missing vowels to reveal the name of the street on which the Conners lived in the show *Roseanne*:

DLWR

Delaware

ANIMATED SERIES
QUESTIONS

1 Which wizard is the sworn enemy of the Smurfs, in the animated TV show *The Smurfs*?

2 What is the name of the female chipmunk band introduced in *Alvin and the Chipmunks*?

3 In the Berenstain Bears TV shows, what type of structure do the bears live in?

4 Dr. Claw is the main antagonist in which originally two-season show based around a cyborg human and his various bionic implements?

5 What type of animal has the turtles' instructor, Splinter, morphed into in the 1987 animated series, *Teenage Mutant Ninja Turtles*?

6 Which Middle Eastern city does Garfield, in *Garfield and Friends*, try again and again to mail a rival tabby, Nermal, to?

7 Rearrange the letters below to reveal the creator of the long-running animated sitcom, *The Simpsons*:

ROTTEN GAMING (4, 8)

ANIMATED SERIES
ANSWERS

1 Which wizard is the sworn enemy of the Smurfs, in the animated TV show *The Smurfs*?

Gargamel

The Smurfs were originally a series of Belgian comics, dating back to the 1950s, soon leading to spin-off merchandise. They later became a successful television series after NBC's president, Fred Silverman, saw that his daughter had a Smurf doll and thought that a show featuring the characters would make a great addition to the channel's Saturday morning line-up.

2 What is the name of the female chipmunk band introduced in *Alvin and the Chipmunks*?

The Chipettes

3 In the Berenstain Bears TV shows, what type of structure do the bears live in?

A tree house

4 Dr. Claw is the main antagonist in which originally two-season show based around a cyborg human and his various bionic implements?

Inspector Gadget

5 What type of animal has the turtles' instructor, Splinter, morphed into in the 1987 animated series, *Teenage Mutant Ninja Turtles*?

Rat—although in one episode he becomes human again

6 Which Middle Eastern city does Garfield, in *Garfield and Friends*, try again and again to mail a rival tabby, Nermal, to?

Abu Dhabi

7 Rearrange the letters below to reveal the creator of the long-running animated sitcom, *The Simpsons*:

ROTTEN GAMING (4, 8)

Matt Groening

CRIME 1
QUESTIONS

1. In *Murder, She Wrote*, from what profession has the lead character, Jessica Fletcher, retired?

2. In which US state is *Magnum P.I.* set?

3. Saundra Santiago played the role of which detective in *Miami Vice*?

4. What is the first name of the titular character in *Inspector Morse*, a show first broadcast in 1987?

5. Rearrange the following letters to reveal which actress originally played Christine Cagney in the pilot movie of *Cagney & Lacey*:

   TOWEL ARTIST (7, 4)

6. What was the name of Virgil Tibbs's hometown in the series, *In the Heat of the Night*?

7. David Suchet first played the title role in *Agatha Christie's Poirot* in which year?

1 In *Murder, She Wrote*, from what profession has the lead character, Jessica Fletcher, retired?

Teaching

> *Murder was such a frequent occurrence within Cabot Cove, a small coastal community that formed the principal location throughout* Murder, She Wrote, *that the term "Cabot Cove syndrome" is now used more generally to describe remote areas in which dead bodies are regularly found.*

2 In which US state is *Magnum P.I.* set?

Hawaii

3 Saundra Santiago played the role of which detective in *Miami Vice*?

Gina Navarro Calabrese

4 What is the first name of the titular character in *Inspector Morse*, a show first broadcast in 1987?

Endeavour

5 Rearrange the following letters to reveal which actress originally played Christine Cagney in the pilot movie of *Cagney & Lacey*:

TOWEL ARTIST (7, 4)

Loretta Swit

6 What was the name of Virgil Tibbs's hometown in the series, *In the Heat of the Night*?

Sparta

7 David Suchet first played the title role in *Agatha Christie's Poirot* in which year?

1989

US SOAPS
QUESTIONS

1. Season 9 of *Dallas* was eventually revealed to have all been entirely a dream of which character?

2. Which woman's name is featured in the title of the theme song for the soap *The Young and the Restless*?

3. In *All My Children*, what was the first name of the character that Liza plotted to win back after he had left her for Jenny?

4. Who were the rival family to the Capwells in *Santa Barbara*?

5. What character did Joan Collins play in the prime time soap opera, *Dynasty*?

6. What name was given to the *Texas* storyline revolving around an ancient Indian artifact named the Fire Compass, which was also the location that key story elements occurred?

7. Rearrange the following letters to reveal the name of the character played by Denise Alexander in *General Hospital*:

   BELLE BY SEWER (6, 6)

1 Season 9 of *Dallas* was eventually revealed to have all been entirely a dream of which character?

Pam(ela) Ewing

Season 9 of Dallas was subsequently referred to as "The Dream Season" or "The Dream Year", with the entire season of episodes dismissed as having all been the fantasy of Pam. The reason for this unusual story decision was so that the previous death of the character Bobby Ewing could be "undone", and then they could return to the show in the hope of resurrecting the falling ratings. Unfortunately the decision was made late in the day, so there were no hints throughout the season that everything was intended to all be a dream.

2 Which woman's name is featured in the title of the theme song for the soap *The Young and the Restless*?

Nadia

3 In *All My Children*, what was the first name of the character that Liza plotted to win back after he had left her for Jenny?

Greg

4 Who were the rival family to the Capwells in *Santa Barbara*?

Lockridge family

5 What character did Joan Collins play in the prime time soap opera, *Dynasty*?

Alexis Carrington Colby

6 What name was given to the *Texas* storyline revolving around an ancient Indian artifact named the Fire Compass, which was also the location that key story elements occurred?

Hitopah

7 Rearrange the following letters to reveal the name of the character played by Denise Alexander in *General Hospital*:

BELLE BY SEWER (6, 6)

Lesley Webber

BRITISH GAME SHOWS
QUESTIONS

1. Who was the original launch presenter of *Countdown*, who went on to present the show for the next 23 years?

2. How many cards were laid out for each team in the Bruce Forsyth show, *Play Your Cards Right*?

3. *Blankety Blank* was based on which American game show with a different name?

4. Cilla Black hosted which popular game show, similar to the shows *Perfect Match* in Australia and *The Dating Game* in the US?

5. Add in the missing vowels, and change the spacing, to reveal the name of the final round in the British version of *The Price is Right*:

   RN GF NDR

6. How many members of the public were surveyed for answers to each of the "everyday questions" in *Family Fortunes*?

7. In the TV show *Catchphrase*, what is the name of the robot mascot who sometimes appear in the animated questions?

BRITISH GAME SHOWS

ANSWERS

1 Who was the original launch presenter of *Countdown*, who went on to present the show for the next 23 years?

Richard Whiteley

Whiteley presented the daily show from 1982 through until his death in 2005, a significant contribution to the fact that he is thought to have spent more time on British TV screens than any other living person, excluding still images of people that appeared on early television test cards.

2 How many cards were laid out for each team in the Bruce Forsyth show, *Play Your Cards Right*?

Five

3 *Blankety Blank* was based on which American game show with a different name?

Match Game

4 Cilla Black hosted which popular game show, similar to the shows *Perfect Match* in Australia and *The Dating Game* in the US?

Blind Date

5 Add in the missing vowels, and change the spacing, to reveal the name of the final round in the British version of *The Price is Right*:

RN GF NDR

Range Finder

6 How many members of the public were surveyed for answers to each of the "everyday questions" in *Family Fortunes*?

100

7 In the TV show *Catchphrase*, what is the name of the robot mascot who sometimes appear in the animated questions?

Mr. Chips

1. Caroll Spinney was best known for playing Big Bird along with which other character on *Sesame Street*?

2. Rearrange the letters below to reveal the character played by Laurence Fishburne in *Pee-wee's Playhouse*:

   TOY CIRCUS BOW (6, 6)

3. What was the name of the bed of flowers, which would provide a joke and punchline on either side of its leaves, in *The Magic Garden*?

4. In *Pinwheel*, what was the name of the alien marionettes that Franci kept in a terrarium?

5. *Against the Odds* was broadcast by which children's cable channel from 1982 to 1984?

6. In which city is the show *Degrassi Junior High* based?

7. What are the four main species within the *Fraggle Rock* environment?

1 Caroll Spinney was best known for playing Big Bird along with which other character on *Sesame Street*?

Oscar the Grouch

Spinney also played Granny Bird, the grandmother to Big Bird, who was in reality a spare Big Bird puppet. He played the roles from the show's beginning in 1969 through until 2018, as well as in a series of cameo appearances by the puppets, including in the film Night at the Museum: Battle of the Smithsonian.

2 Rearrange the letters below to reveal the character played by Laurence Fishburne in *Pee-wee's Playhouse*:

TOY CIRCUS BOW (6, 6)

Cowboy Curtis

3 What was the name of the bed of flowers, which would provide a joke and punchline on either side of its leaves, in *The Magic Garden*?

Chuckle Patch

4 In *Pinwheel*, what was the name of the alien marionettes that Franci kept in a terrarium?

Wonkles

5 *Against the Odds* was broadcast by which children's cable channel from 1982 to 1984?

Nickelodeon

6 In which city is the show *Degrassi Junior High* based?

Toronto

7 What are the four main species within the *Fraggle Rock* environment?

Doozers, Gorgs, Fraggles, and Silly Creatures

SATURDAY NIGHT LIVE 1
QUESTIONS

1. Which writer did Julia Louis-Dreyfus meet on her final year at *SNL*, who would later co-write Seinfeld?

2. What character did Eddie Murphy play on *SNL* that parodied long-running children's presenter Mister Rogers?

3. "You look... mahvelous!" was the catchphrase spoken by which cast member, imitating playboy actor Fernando Lamas?

4. After how many episodes did Ben Stiller leave *SNL*?

   a. 1
   b. 4
   c. 14
   d. 40

5. Who was the first female *SNL* cast member to have been born outside of North America?

6. In which year did Laurie Metcalf appear as a cast member on *SNL* for the one and only time, earning her a record for the shortest cast tenure of anyone who actually appeared on screen?

7. Which *SNL* performer played the reoccurring character of Dieter, the host of *Sprockets*, who parodied 1980s German culture?

1 Which writer did Julia Louis-Dreyfus meet on her final year at *SNL*, who would later co-write Seinfeld?

Larry David

Julia Louis-Dreyfus became SNL's youngest ever cast member when she joined the show at the age of just 21 in 1982, while still a theater student at Northwestern University. She remained a cast member until 1985. She also married one of her fellow cast members, Brad Hall.

2 What character did Eddie Murphy play on *SNL* that parodied long-running children's presenter Mister Rogers?

Mister Robinson

3 "You look... mahvelous!" was the catchphrase spoken by which cast member, imitating playboy actor Fernando Lamas?

Billy Crystal

4 After how many episodes did Ben Stiller leave *SNL*?

a. 1
b. 4
c. 14
d. 40

b. 4

5 Who was the first female *SNL* cast member to have been born outside of North America?

Pamela Stephenson

6 In which year did Laurie Metcalf appear as a cast member on *SNL* for the one and only time, earning her a record for the shortest cast tenure of anyone who actually appeared on screen?

1981

7 Which *SNL* performer played the reoccurring character of Dieter, the host of *Sprockets*, who parodied 1980s German culture?

Mike Myers

NEW CHANNELS
QUESTIONS

1 A montage of which historical event was used as part of the the 1981 on-air launch of MTV?

2 Which musical term was part of a previous name of what is now known as CNBC?

3 Which Disney character featured in the title of Disney Channel's first original series?

4 Which was the very first music video broadcast on MTV?

5 Which was the first 24-hours-a-day television news network?

6 In 1988, The Discovery Channel began an annual tradition of basing a week's worth of programming around which ferocious animal?

7 Which US television and radio broadcaster is sometimes referred to as the "Peacock Network"?

1 A montage of which historical event was used as part of the the 1981 on-air launch of MTV?

The *Apollo 11* moon landing

> *Originally there were plans to include the famous "One small step" quote in the broadcast, but Neil Armstrong refused permission so a beeping noise was played instead. The montage also showed the Space Shuttle Colombia launch from April of the same year.*

2 Which musical term was part of a previous name of what is now known as CNBC?

Tempo—before becoming CNBC it was known as Tempo Television

3 Which Disney character featured in the title of Disney Channel's first original series?

Mickey—in *Good Morning, Mickey!*

4 Which was the very first music video broadcast on MTV?

The Buggles's *Video Killed the Radio Star*

5 Which was the first 24-hours-a-day television news network?

Cable News Network (CNN)

6 In 1988, The Discovery Channel began an annual tradition of basing a week's worth of programming around which ferocious animal?

The shark

7 Which US television and radio broadcaster is sometimes referred to as the "Peacock Network"?

NBC

BRITISH SOAPS
QUESTIONS

1. In which fictional square is the long-running British soap *Eastenders* set?

2. In *Crossroads*, what was the relation between the characters Kitty and Meg, whose feud formed part of the original premise of the show?

3. In which year did *Emmerdale Farm*, a soap set in a fictional village in the Yorkshire Dales, change its name to just *Emmerdale*?

4. *Angels* was a British soap, last broadcast in 1983, that centered around which profession?

5. In which fictional town is the world's longest-running television soap opera, *Coronation Street*, set?

6. Rearrange the following letters to reveal the soap which had the first openly gay character in a British television series:

   DIRE BOOKS (9)

7. How many main characters were in the first series of *Casualty*, all introduced in the opening episode?

   a. 5
   b. 10
   c. 15
   d. 20

1 In which fictional square is the long-running British soap *Eastenders* set?

Albert Square

According to the show, the Square is in the E20 London postcode area, and connects to Bridge Street, Victoria Road, and Turpin Way. The set for the Square was one of the largest ever created for a British TV show, and had to be designed to last for many years. The effort was rewarded, however, when the first episode of Eastenders *attracted around 17 million viewers, and the show has been broadcast continuously since its 1985 launch.*

2 In *Crossroads*, what was the relation between the characters Kitty and Meg, whose feud formed part of the original premise of the show?

Sisters

3 In which year did *Emmerdale Farm*, a soap set in a fictional village in the Yorkshire Dales, change its name to just *Emmerdale*?

1989

4 *Angels* was a British soap, last broadcast in 1983, that centered around which profession?

Nursing

5 In which fictional town is the world's longest-running television soap opera, *Coronation Street*, set?

Weatherfield, based on inner-city Salford

6 Rearrange the following letters to reveal the soap which had the first openly gay character in a British television series:

DIRE BOOKS (9)

Brookside

7 How many main characters were in the first series of *Casualty*, all introduced in the opening episode?

a. 5
b. 10
c. 15
d. 20

b. 10

TALK SHOWS
QUESTIONS

1. What half-hour talk show was renamed to *The Oprah Winfrey Show*, a year after Oprah took it over in 1984?

2. Which famous pop artist hosted a talk show on MTV from 1985 to 1987?

3. How many minutes did *The David Letterman Show* originally last?

4. Which father of a former New York governor and a former CNN anchor was Larry King's first guest on *Larry King Live*?

5. In which year did President Jimmy Carter appear on *Meet the Press* to announce the US boycott of the summer Olympics?

6. What colors were on the necktie that Wally George wore to host his talk show, *Hot Seat*?

7. In which year did *The Joan Rivers Show* premiere, which went on to air for five seasons?

1 What half-hour talk show was renamed to *The Oprah Winfrey Show*, a year after Oprah took it over in 1984?

A.M. Chicago

The talk show aired on WLS-TV, a Chicago station. After Oprah took over the show in January 1984, it went to first place in the local Chicago TV ratings, leading to the renaming. But it was Oprah's performance in the movie The Color Purple *that led to its national launch.* The Oprah Winfrey Show *eventually went on to receive 47 Emmy Awards before Oprah ceased submitting it for consideration.*

2 Which famous pop artist hosted a talk show on MTV from 1985 to 1987?

Andy Warhol

3 How many minutes did *The David Letterman Show* originally last?

90

4 Which father of a former New York governor and a former CNN anchor was Larry King's first guest on *Larry King Live*?

Mario Cuomo

5 In which year did President Jimmy Carter appear on *Meet the Press* to announce the US boycott of the summer Olympics?

1980

6 What colors were on the necktie that Wally George wore to host his talk show, *Hot Seat*?

Red, white, and blue

7 In which year did *The Joan Rivers Show* premiere, which went on to air for five seasons?

1989

US GAME SHOWS
QUESTIONS

1. What was the name of the NBC game show that aired from 1980 to 1982, featuring three spinning windows that needed to be stopped by hitting a plunger?

2. In *Family Feud*, how many opposing contestants take part in the "face-off" question?

3. Who hosted *The (New) $25,000 Pyramid* from 1982 to 1988?

4. Restore the missing vowels, and change the spacing, to reveal the Mexican-American comedian who presented *The Newlywed Game* from 1988 to 1989:

   P LRD RG Z

5. *Hollywood Squares* returned to NBC in 1983 as one half of an hour-long hybrid show that saw it paired up with which other game show?

6. Which game show of the 1980s was known for the "Whammy", a red creature that appeared in certain spaces?

7. What was the minimum age for audience members changed to in 1988, for *The Price Is Right*?

1 What was the name of the NBC game show that aired from 1980 to 1982, featuring three spinning windows that needed to be stopped by hitting a plunger?

Bullseye

The show ran for 390 episodes, with the generous feature that all contestants won whatever money they banked during the game, irrespective of whether they eventually won or lost the show. Contestants who won more than once would win a car after their fifth victory. The show was later renamed to Celebrity Bullseye, *featuring contestants that included actress Lynn Redgrave.*

2 In *Family Feud*, how many opposing contestants take part in the "face-off" question?

2

3 Who hosted *The (New) $25,000 Pyramid* from 1982 to 1988?

Dick Clark

4 Restore the missing vowels, and change the spacing, to reveal the Mexican-American comedian who presented *The Newlywed Game* from 1988 to 1989:

P LRD RG Z

Paul Rodriguez

5 *Hollywood Squares* returned to NBC in 1983 as one half of an hour-long hybrid show that saw it paired up with which other game show?

Match Game

6 Which game show of the 1980s was known for the "Whammy", a red creature that appeared in certain spaces?

Press Your Luck

7 What was the minimum age for audience members changed to in 1988, for *The Price Is Right*?

18—prior to then, children could attend

DALLAS
QUESTIONS

1. In *Dallas*, what nickname was given to the character of Willard Barnes?

2. What was the last name of the affluent but feuding family that *Dallas* revolves around?

3. Which family were the main rivals to the Ewing family in *Dallas*?

4. The show's creator, David Jacobs, originally envisaged a more middle-class cast of characters, but the network wanted to make the show more "glitzy". What was the name of the *Dallas* spin-off he subsequently created, which stuck more to his original vision?

5. Rearrange the following letters to reveal the actress who played the *Dallas* family matriarch, Eleanor "Miss Ellie" Ewing Farlow?

   DEAR AGED BABBLERS (7, 3, 6)

6. Who was the only character to appear in every episode of the original *Dallas*?

7. Who was the daughter of Gary Ewing and Valene Clements in *Dallas*?

1 In *Dallas*, what nickname was given to the character of Willard Barnes?

Digger

> *David Wayne played the role of Willard "Digger" Barnes in the first two seasons of Dallas, but was unable to continue due to a co-starring role in the CBS series, House Calls, so he was replaced by his friend Keenan Wynn for season 3, in 1980.*

2 What was the last name of the affluent but feuding family that *Dallas* revolves around?

Ewing

3 Which family were the main rivals to the Ewing family in *Dallas*?

The Barnes family

4 The show's creator, David Jacobs, originally envisaged a more middle-class cast of characters, but the network wanted to make the show more "glitzy". What was the name of the *Dallas* spin-off he subsequently created, which stuck more to his original vision?

Knots Landing

5 Rearrange the following letters to reveal the actress who played the *Dallas* family matriarch, Eleanor "Miss Ellie" Ewing Farlow?

DEAR AGED BABBLERS (7, 3, 6)

Barbara Bel Geddes

6 Who was the only character to appear in every episode of the original *Dallas*?

J. R., a.k.a. John Ross Ewing Jr.

7 Who was the daughter of Gary Ewing and Valene Clements in *Dallas*?

Lucy

TELEVISED EVENTS
QUESTIONS

1 Which event, broadcast on July 29, 1981, is thought to have been watched by 750 million people worldwide?

2 Bob Geldof and which other singer-songwriter were responsible for organizing the original *Live Aid* concert, broadcast to raise money for the tragic famine in Ethiopia?

3 In which year did *Saturday Night Live* celebrate its 15th Anniversary Special with a tribute show?

4 Which two people hosted the first ever *MTV Video Music Awards*, in 1984?

5 The Space Shuttle *Challenger* disaster of 1986 was broadcast live on which network?

6 Michael Jackson won eight Grammy awards in 1984, including for *Thriller*, watched by a television audience of how many viewers?

a. About 22 million
b. About 32 million
c. About 42 million
d. About 52 million

7 Rearrange the following letters to reveal the game show on which Michael Larson won cash and items worth a total of $110,237 in 1984, at that point the highest one-day total ever given away on a game show:

SURE LUCKY PROS (5, 4, 4)

1 Which event, broadcast on July 29, 1981, is thought to have been watched by 750 million people worldwide?

The wedding of Prince Charles and Lady Diana Spencer

The largest TV audience for a wedding of all time, the broadcast was aired in 74 different countries, with almost thirty million watching it in the UK alone. Diana's untimely death in 1997, however, led to a funeral that is thought to have been watched by a staggering 2.5 billion people worldwide—that's one in three people on the planet.

2 Bob Geldof and which other singer-songwriter were responsible for organizing the original *Live Aid* concert, broadcast to raise money for the tragic famine in Ethiopia?

Midge Ure

3 In which year did *Saturday Night Live* celebrate its 15th Anniversary Special with a tribute show?

1989

4 Which two people hosted the first ever *MTV Video Music Awards*, in 1984?

Dan Aykroyd and Bette Midler

5 The Space Shuttle *Challenger* disaster of 1986 was broadcast live on which network?

CNN

6 Michael Jackson won eight Grammy awards in 1984, including for *Thriller*, watched by a television audience of how many viewers?

a. About 22 million
b. About 32 million
c. About 42 million
d. About 52 million

d. About 52 million

7 Rearrange the following letters to reveal the game show on which Michael Larson won cash and items worth a total of $110,237 in 1984, at that point the highest one-day total ever given away on a game show:

SURE LUCKY PROS (5, 4, 4)

Press Your Luck

POT LUCK 1
QUESTIONS

1. By what nickname was Sergeant Bosco Baracus better known in *The A-Team*?

2. Which actor played the role of the Doctor in *Doctor Who* from 1984 to 1986?

3. What was the name of the pet squirrel that featured in the series *The Joy of Painting*, hosted by painter Bob Ross?

4. The last season of the original *Charlie's Angels* was broadcast from 1980 to 1981, but what was notable about the title of the penultimate episode of the season, compared to the rest of that season's titles?

5. What food was used to demonstrate the effect of drugs during the large-scale US anti-narcotics campaign, *This Is Your Brain on Drugs*?

6. Who rose to prominence as a teen idol when they were cast in the role of Tom Hanson in the *21 Jump Street* TV series?

7. After *Airwolf* was canceled by CBS after three seasons, which cable channel picked it up for a fourth-season renewal?

1 By what nickname was Sergeant Bosco Baracus better known in *The A-Team*?

"B.A." Baracus

The role of B.A. Baracus was written especially for Mr. T, a professional wrestler known for his gold neck chains and other jewelry, and who had become a bodyguard for celebrities that included Muhammad Ali, Steve McQueen, and Michael Jackson. The character was famous for his catchphrase, "I pity the fool", despite it never actually being spoken on the show—it was in fact in another of his roles, in Rocky III, that Mr. T spoke the famous line.

2 Which actor played the role of the Doctor in *Doctor Who* from 1984 to 1986?

Colin Baker

3 What was the name of the pet squirrel that featured in the series *The Joy of Painting*, hosted by painter Bob Ross?

Peapod

4 The last season of the original *Charlie's Angels* was broadcast from 1980 to 1981, but what was notable about the title of the penultimate episode of the season, compared to the rest of that season's titles?

It was the only one without the word "Angel" or "Angels" in its title

5 What food was used to demonstrate the effect of drugs during the large-scale US anti-narcotics campaign, *This Is Your Brain on Drugs*?

Eggs (cooking in a frying pan)

6 Who rose to prominence as a teen idol when they were cast in the role of Tom Hanson in the *21 Jump Street* TV series?

Johnny Depp

7 After *Airwolf* was canceled by CBS after three seasons, which cable channel picked it up for a fourth-season renewal?

USA Network

BRITISH KIDS TV
QUESTIONS

1 In the stop-motion animated TV series, *Postman Pat*, what is the occupation of the character Mrs. Goggins?

2 In their eponymous series, what was the name of the Chuckle Brothers' main form of transport?

3 Which comic actor voiced the character of Danger Mouse in the 1981 television series of the same name?

4 What is the central feature of the logo for the long-running television show, *Blue Peter*?

5 Which is the title of the song that features in the 1982 animation, *The Snowman*?

6 *Fireman Sam* is set in the fictional Welsh village of Pontypandy, which combines the names of which two real Welsh towns?

7 Restore the missing vowels to reveal the name of the fictional island on which *Thomas the Tank Engine & Friends* is set:

SDR

1 In the stop-motion animated TV series, *Postman Pat*, what is the occupation of the character Mrs. Goggins?

Postmistress

Postman Pat's creator, John Cunliffe, said that he chose the occupation of postman as he needed someone that could travel to a range of locations in order to interact with lots of different characters. The post office itself was inspired by one previously located in the street he lived in while writing the series.

2 In their eponymous series, what was the name of the Chuckle Brothers' main form of transport?

Chuckmobile

3 Which comic actor voiced the character of Danger Mouse in the 1981 television series of the same name?

David Jason

4 What is the central feature of the logo for the long-running television show, *Blue Peter*?

A sailing ship

5 Which is the title of the song that features in the 1982 animation, *The Snowman*?

Walking in the Air

6 *Fireman Sam* is set in the fictional Welsh village of Pontypandy, which combines the names of which two real Welsh towns?

Pontypridd and Tonypandy

7 Restore the missing vowels to reveal the name of the fictional island on which *Thomas the Tank Engine & Friends* is set:

SDR

Sodor

AWARD-WINNING SHOWS
QUESTIONS

1. Throughout its run, *Taxi* won a staggering 18 Emmy Awards, all but three of them in the 1980s. What is the name of the fictional cab company that the series centers on?

2. Who won two Lead Actress in a Comedy Series Emmys, in both 1984 and 1985, for her role as Allison "Allie" Lowell in *Kate & Allie*?

3. *Barney Miller* was a sitcom set in a New York City police department that ran from 1975 until which year of the 1980s?

4. In which year did *Thirtysomething* win the Emmy Award for Outstanding Drama Series?

5. In which city is medical drama *St. Elsewhere*, the winner of thirteen Emmys, set?

6. *The Wonder Years* covered which years in the life of stereotypical American boy, Kevin, making its star the youngest-ever nominee for the Outstanding Lead Actor in a Comedy Series Emmy?

7. The license plate shown in the series title of *L.A. Law*, with the registration "LA Law", was shown on what make of car for the show's first seven seasons?

AWARD-WINNING SHOWS

ANSWERS

1 Throughout its run, *Taxi* won a staggering 18 Emmy Awards, all but three of them in the 1980s. What is the name of the fictional cab company that the series centers on?

Sunshine Cab Company

Among those winning Emmys for their work on the show were Danny DeVito, who won for Supporting Actor in a Comedy Series in 1981, and Christopher Lloyd, who won the same award in 1982 and 1983. It also won four Golden Globes.

2 Who won two Lead Actress in a Comedy Series Emmys, in both 1984 and 1985, for her role as Allison "Allie" Lowell in *Kate & Allie*?

Jane Curtin

3 *Barney Miller* was a sitcom set in a New York City police department that ran from 1975 until which year of the 1980s?

1982

4 In which year did *Thirtysomething* win the Emmy Award for Outstanding Drama Series?

1988

5 In which city is medical drama *St. Elsewhere*, the winner of thirteen Emmys, set?

Boston

6 *The Wonder Years* covered which years in the life of stereotypical American boy, Kevin, making its star the youngest-ever nominee for the Outstanding Lead Actor in a Comedy Series Emmy?

12 to 17

7 The license plate shown in the series title of *L.A. Law*, with the registration "LA Law", was shown on what make of car for the show's first seven seasons?

Jaguar—later, in the final season, it was on a Bentley

TV THEME TUNES
QUESTIONS

1 Which 1980s TV show featured *Where Everybody Knows Your Name* as its opening theme?

2 Rearrange the following letters to reveal the songwriter who wrote *Thank You for Being a Friend*, used as the theme tune for *The Golden Girls*:

GLARED DOWN (6, 4)

3 Who sang the theme tune for long-running children's series, *Reading Rainbow*, throughout the 1980s and most of the subsequent decade too?

4 *Unknown Stuntman* is the opening theme to action series *The Fall Guy* and was sung by which well-known actor?

5 Which opening theme song to a TV show of the same name, starring Bruce Willis and Cybill Shepherd, was nominated for two Grammys in 1988?

6 *Everywhere You Look* is the theme song to which sitcom that first aired in 1987?

7 Bill Conti composed the opening theme to *Dynasty*, as well as the score to which 1983 historical drama movie?

TV THEME TUNES
ANSWERS

1 Which 1980s TV show featured *Where Everybody Knows Your Name* as its opening theme?

Cheers

After the successful premiere of Cheers, a longer version was recorded that made the charts in both the US and Britain. The song was also nominated for the 1983 Emmy for Outstanding Achievement in Music and Lyrics, and has since been voted the best television theme of all time by readers of Rolling Stone magazine.

2 Rearrange the following letters to reveal the songwriter who wrote *Thank You for Being a Friend*, used as the theme tune for *The Golden Girls*:

GLARED DOWN (6, 4)

Andrew Gold

3 Who sang the theme tune for long-running children's series, *Reading Rainbow*, throughout the 1980s and most of the subsequent decade too?

Tina Fabrique

4 *Unknown Stuntman* is the opening theme to action series *The Fall Guy* and was sung by which well-known actor?

Lee Majors

5 Which opening theme song to a TV show of the same name, starring Bruce Willis and Cybill Shepherd, was nominated for two Grammys in 1988?

Moonlighting

6 *Everywhere You Look* is the theme song to which sitcom that first aired in 1987?

Full House

7 Bill Conti composed the opening theme to *Dynasty*, as well as the score to which 1983 historical drama movie?

The Right Stuff

SATURDAY NIGHT LIVE 2
QUESTIONS

1 From which studio of the Comcast Building is *SNL* broadcast?

2 Which sketch, featuring the character of Garth Algar, first appeared in a 1989 episode of *SNL*?

3 Which actor, nominated for Emmy awards for his first two years on the show, played the reoccurring character of Mephistopheles on *SNL*?

4 Why was Damon Wayans fired from *SNL*, in 1986?

5 How old was Drew Barrymore when she first hosted *SNL*, on November 20, 1982?

6 Add in the missing vowels and change the spacing to reveal the prominent *SNL* performer who became, in 1982, the only cast member to host the show while still a regular:

D DMR P HY

7 Who performed the songs *Caribbean Queen* and *Loverboy* on the *SNL* episode of January 19, 1985, also performing the same two songs as part of *Live Aid* later that year?

SATURDAY NIGHT LIVE 2

ANSWERS

1 From which studio of the Comcast Building is *SNL* broadcast?

8H

> The building is also the headquarters of SNL broadcaster NBC, and is located at 30 Rockefeller Plaza in New York City. Due to its street address, it's sometimes referred to as "30 Rock", which eventually led to a NBC sitcom of the same name.

2 Which sketch, featuring the character of Garth Algar, first appeared in a 1989 episode of *SNL*?

Wayne's World

3 Which actor, nominated for Emmy awards for his first two years on the show, played the reoccurring character of Mephistopheles on *SNL*?

Jon Lovitz

4 Why was Damon Wayans fired from *SNL*, in 1986?

He "sabotaged" a scene by playing a character very differently to how it had been written

5 How old was Drew Barrymore when she first hosted *SNL*, on November 20, 1982?

7

6 Add in the missing vowels and change the spacing to reveal the prominent *SNL* performer who became, in 1982, the only cast member to host the show while still a regular:

D DMR P HY

Eddie Murphy

7 Who performed the songs *Caribbean Queen* and *Loverboy* on the *SNL* episode of January 19, 1985, also performing the same two songs in *Live Aid* later that year?

Billy Ocean

DYNASTY
QUESTIONS

1. How many seasons were there during the original 1980s run of *Dynasty*?

2. Costume designer Nolan Miller said of the characters in the show that he would "never want to see them wearing the same outfit twice". To the nearest thousand, how many costumes did he make over the course of *Dynasty*?

3. Joan Collins joined the cast of *Dynasty* in its second season, playing which character that transformed the actress into an international star?

4. The original premiere event on ABC for *Dynasty* lasted how many hours?

   a. 1 hour
   b. 2 hours
   c. 3 hours
   d. 4 hours

5. Based on its intention to be a direct competitor to *Dallas*, what working title was used during the development of *Dynasty*?

6. In which year did *Dynasty* win a Golden Globe Award for Best TV Drama Series?

7. In which US state was *Dynasty* filmed?

1 How many seasons were there during the original 1980s run of *Dynasty*?

Nine

The show ran from 1981 to 1989, with 220 episodes in total, but eventually ended on a cliffhanger, to the dissatisfaction of many. A two-part miniseries entitled Dynasty: The Reunion *eventually aired a couple of years later as an attempt to tie up the various loose ends.*

2 Costume designer Nolan Miller said of the characters in the show that he would "never want to see them wearing the same outfit twice". To the nearest thousand, how many costumes did he make over the course of *Dynasty*?

3,000

3 Joan Collins joined the cast of *Dynasty* in its second season, playing which character that transformed the actress into an international star?

Alexis Carrington Colby

4 The original premiere event on ABC for *Dynasty* lasted how many hours?

a. 1 hour
b. 2 hours
c. 3 hours
d. 4 hours

c. 3 hours

5 Based on its intention to be a direct competitor to *Dallas*, what working title was used during the development of *Dynasty*?

Oil

6 In which year did *Dynasty* win a Golden Globe Award for Best TV Drama Series?

1983

7 In which US state was *Dynasty* filmed?

California

CRIME 2
QUESTIONS

1. What was the name of Michael Knight's speaking, intelligent car in *Knight Rider*?

2. What was Columbo's oft-repeated catchphrase, in the show of the same name?

3. What was the name of the restaurant and lounge owned by Val Bisoglio's character in *Quincy M.E.*?

4. *Hill Street Blues* received a large number of Emmy awards in its debut season, but how many exactly?

   a. 4
   b. 6
   c. 8
   d. 10

5. As well as "the Agency", what other name was used for the US government intelligence organization that Robert McCall used to work for, in *The Equalizer*?

6. What was character Steve McGarrett's title within the Five-O Task force, in the show *Hawaii Five-O*?

7. Which two actors starred as the private detectives Maddie Hayes and David Addison in *Moonlighting*?

1 What was the name of Michael Knight's speaking, intelligent car in *Knight Rider*?

KITT

> *KITT, short for "Knight Industries Two Thousand", was voiced on-screen by William Daniels, who asked not to be credited in the show's opening titles so that the car could be felt to have a voice of its own, rather than someone else's. He was, however, credited in the closing titles.*

2 What was Columbo's oft-repeated catchphrase, in the show of the same name?

"Just one more thing"

3 What was the name of the restaurant and lounge owned by Val Bisoglio's character in *Quincy M.E.*?

Danny's

4 *Hill Street Blues* received a large number of Emmy awards in its debut season, but how many exactly?

a. 4
b. 6
c. 8
d. 10

c. 8

5 As well as "the Agency", what other name was used for the US government intelligence organization that Robert McCall used to work for, in *The Equalizer*?

The Company

6 What was character Steve McGarrett's title within the Five-O Task force, in the show *Hawaii Five-O*?

Commander

7 Which two actors starred as the private detectives Maddie Hayes and David Addison in *Moonlighting*?

Cybill Shepherd and Bruce Willis

SPORTS
QUESTIONS

1 What was the final score in the 1980 Winter Olympics ice hockey game known as the *Miracle on Ice*, when the United States beat the Soviet Union?

2 What ultimately caused the disruption of game three during the Major League Baseball 1989 World Series?

3 After how many failed attempts did Darrell Waltrip finally win the *Daytona 500*, in 1989, in a car of the same number?

4 Rearrange the letters below to reveal the name of the commentator, a former Celtics player, who accompanied Dick Stockton to cover the 1987 NBA Final between the Los Angeles Lakers and the Boston Celtics?

MONTH IN SHOE (3, 8)

5 ABC paid what then-record amount of money to broadcast the 1984 summer Olympic Games, held in Los Angeles?

a. $125 million
b. $175 million
c. $225 million
d. $275 million

6 How many successive matches, over multiple years, had Björn Borg won at Wimbledon before being defeated by John McEnroe in 1981?

7 Which computer company paid for possibly the most famous Super Bowl commercial of all time, an Orwellian themed ad broadcast during the 1984 event?

1 What was the final score in the 1980 Winter Olympics ice hockey game known as the *Miracle on Ice*, when the United States beat the Soviet Union?

4–3 to the US

> *The Soviet Union had won five of the previous six gold medals in the event so were favorites to win, especially because their team contained mostly professional players as opposed to the primarily amateur team that the US was fielding. The event gained its nickname after the US broadcast commentator, Al Michaels, closed out the game by saying "Do you believe in miracles? Yes!".*

2 What ultimately caused the disruption of game three during the Major League Baseball 1989 World Series?

The Loma Prieta earthquake

3 After how many failed attempts did Darrell Waltrip finally win the *Daytona 500*, in 1989, in a car of the same number?

17

4 Rearrange the letters below to reveal the name of the commentator, a former Celtics player, who accompanied Dick Stockton to cover the 1987 NBA Final between the Los Angeles Lakers and the Boston Celtics?

MONTH IN SHOE (3, 8)

Tom Heinsohn

5 ABC paid what then-record amount of money to broadcast the 1984 summer Olympic Games, held in Los Angeles?

a. $125 million
b. $175 million
c. $225 million
d. $275 million

c. $225 million

6 How many successive matches, over multiple years, had Björn Borg won at Wimbledon before being defeated by John McEnroe in 1981?

41

7 Which computer company paid for possibly the most famous Super Bowl commercial of all time, an Orwellian themed ad broadcast during the 1984 event?

Apple

BRITISH COMEDY
QUESTIONS

1. After the actor who played Grandad died, which character was written into *Only Fools and Horses* as a direct replacement?

2. Which fictional government department does the main character, Jim Hacker, work for in *Yes Minister*?

3. Rearrange the following letters to reveal the codename of René Artois in *'Allo 'Allo!*:

   THANK WHIG (9)

4. In the anarchic comedy *The Young Ones*, what was the name of Vyvyan's hamster?

5. In the sitcom *Open All Hours*, what relation is Granville to Albert Arkwright?

6. Which British comedy is centered on Dave Lister, who wakes up 3 million years in the future, in space, and discovers he is the last human alive?

7. Each season of *Blackadder* moves forward in time, but in what year is the first season of *Blackadder* set?

BRITISH COMEDY
ANSWERS

1 After the actor who played Grandad died, which character was written into *Only Fools and Horses* as a direct replacement?

Uncle Albert

Actor Lennard Pearce played the role of Del and Rodney's Grandad in the first three series of the show, but after his death in 1984 he was replaced with the character of Uncle Albert, played by the actor Buster Merryfield. Running for seven series, plus a large number of Christmas specials, Only Fools and Horses had a significant influence on British culture, including popularizing the insult "plonker" and the phrase "lovely jubbly".

2 Which fictional government department does the main character, Jim Hacker, work for in *Yes Minister*?

Department of Administrative Affairs

3 Rearrange the following letters to reveal the codename of René Artois in *'Allo 'Allo!*:

THANK WHIG (9)

Nighthawk

4 In the anarchic comedy *The Young Ones*, what was the name of Vyvyan's hamster?

Special Patrol Group (SPG)

5 In the sitcom *Open All Hours*, what relation is Granville to Albert Arkwright?

Nephew

6 Which British comedy is centered on Dave Lister, who wakes up 3 million years in the future, in space, and discovers he is the last human alive?

Red Dwarf

7 Each season of *Blackadder* moves forward in time, but in what year is the first season of *Blackadder* set?

1485

OPRAH
QUESTIONS

1. For its first nationally broadcast episode, which *Miami Vice* actor did *The Oprah Winfrey Show* repeatedly try to book as its first guest?

2. In the show's second season, Oprah had what she later described as her worst-ever interviewing experience with which seven-times married actress?

3. Which American pianist, singer, and actor performed on *The Oprah Winfrey Show* on Christmas Day, 1986, causing Oprah to exclaim that it was "the most beautiful medley I've ever heard"?

4. What was the name of the segment of *The Oprah Winfrey Show* which showcased ordinary people who had experienced extraordinary events?

5. How many times did Celine Dion appear on *The Oprah Winfrey Show* in total?
   a. 7
   b. 17
   c. 22
   d. 27

6. How many seasons of *The Oprah Winfrey Show* were produced for national broadcast?

7. Oprah founded her own production company in 1986, under what name that was closely related to her own?

1 For its first nationally broadcast episode, which *Miami Vice* actor did *The Oprah Winfrey Show* repeatedly try to book as its first guest?

Don Johnson

The show tried offering him various gifts as an enticement to appear, including rhinestone glasses and Dom Pérignon, but without success. Oprah decided instead to make the show about everyday people, choosing the theme for that first show of "How to Marry the Man or Woman of Your Choice".

2 In the show's second season, Oprah had what she later described as her worst-ever interviewing experience with which seven-times married actress?

Elizabeth Taylor

3 Which American pianist, singer, and actor performed on *The Oprah Winfrey Show* on Christmas Day, 1986, causing Oprah to exclaim that it was "the most beautiful medley I've ever heard"?

Liberace

4 What was the name of the segment of *The Oprah Winfrey Show* which showcased ordinary people who had experienced extraordinary events?

Remembering Your Spirit

5 How many times did Celine Dion appear on *The Oprah Winfrey Show* in total?

a. 7
b. 17
c. 22
d. 27

d. 27

6 How many seasons of *The Oprah Winfrey Show* were produced for national broadcast?

25

7 Oprah founded her own production company in 1986, under what name that was closely related to her own?

Harpo Productions—"Harpo" is "Oprah" written backwards

POT LUCK 2
QUESTIONS

1. The first season of *Roseanne* aired from 1988 to 1989, with the character of Roseanne played by the actress Roseanne Barr—but what was the surname of the on-screen character?

2. Regina King starred as which character in the sitcom *227*, named after the apartment building it is set in?

3. Which US sitcom introduced the characters of Tony Micelli, a former baseball player, and Angela Bower, for whom he becomes a live-in housekeeper?

4. What are the names of the parents of Ben, Carol, and Mike in *Growing Pains*, first aired in 1985?

5. In the *Dukes of Hazzard*, which ended in 1985 after seven seasons, who played the role of Daisy Duke?

6. For how many seasons was the show *Happy Days* broadcast before it finally came to an end in 1984?

7. What is the occupation of Ben Matlock in the series of the same name, *Matlock*?

1. The first season of *Roseanne* aired from 1988 to 1989, with the character of Roseanne played by the actress Roseanne Barr—but what was the surname of the on-screen character?

Conner (née Harris)

> *Barr had worked as a stand-up comedian throughout the 1980s, becoming so successful that ABC offered her her own series. The first episode was watched by over 21 million households, making it the most successful debut show of the season. The show also later became the first staff writing job for Joss Whedon.*

2. Regina King starred as which character in the sitcom *227*, named after the apartment building it is set in?

Brenda

3. Which US sitcom introduced the characters of Tony Micelli, a former baseball player, and Angela Bower, for whom he becomes a live-in housekeeper?

Who's the Boss?

4. What are the names of the parents of Ben, Carol, and Mike in *Growing Pains*, first aired in 1985?

Jason and Maggie (Margaret)

5. In the *Dukes of Hazzard*, which ended in 1985 after seven seasons, who played the role of Daisy Duke?

Catherine Bach

6. For how many seasons was the show *Happy Days* broadcast before it finally came to an end in 1984?

Eleven

7. What is the occupation of Ben Matlock in the series of the same name, *Matlock*?

Defense attorney

JEOPARDY!
QUESTIONS

1. In what year did the daily syndicated version of *Jeopardy!* premiere, with Alex Trebek as host?

2. What is unusual about the format in which *Jeopardy!* contestants must give their answers?

3. How many clues are given during the Final Jeopardy! round?

4. What name is given to the strategy, coined after the last name of a 1985 contestant who retired unbeaten with then-record winnings of $72,800, that was designed to confuse opponents by rapidly changing category during the Jeopardy! and Double Jeopardy! rounds?

5. Which song is used for the 30-second Final Jeopardy! period in which contestants write down their answers, and also since 1984 for the main titles? It was originally composed as a lullaby for the son of the creator, Merv Griffin.

6. From 1985, the backgrounds were blue for Jeopardy! round, but what color were they for the Double Jeopardy! and Final Jeopardy! rounds?

7. From what date were contestants forced to wait for each clue to be read out in full before ringing in with their response?

1 In what year did the daily syndicated version of *Jeopardy!* premiere, with Alex Trebek as host?

1984

Trebek became host when the show was revived in 1984, and went on to present it for 37 seasons until his death in 2020, winning the Daytime Emmy Award for Outstanding Game Show Host eight times during that time. The only exception was when he switched with the host of Wheel of Fortune, *Pat Sajak, as an April Fool's joke.*

2 What is unusual about the format in which *Jeopardy!* contestants must give their answers?

They must be phrased as a question that results in the given word or phrase

3 How many clues are given during the Final Jeopardy! round?

1

4 What name is given to the strategy, coined after the last name of a 1985 contestant who retired unbeaten with then-record winnings of $72,800, that was designed to confuse opponents by rapidly changing category during the Jeopardy! and Double Jeopardy! rounds?

Forrest Bounce, named after Chuck Forrest

5 Which song is used for the 30-second Final Jeopardy! period in which contestants write down their answers, and also since 1984 for the main titles? It was originally composed as a lullaby for the son of the creator, Merv Griffin.

Think!

6 From 1985, the backgrounds were blue for Jeopardy! round, but what color were they for the Double Jeopardy! and Final Jeopardy! rounds?

Red

7 From what date were contestants forced to wait for each clue to be read out in full before ringing in with their response?

September 1985

MUSIC

The 80s music video scene might not have killed the radio star, but they made the disco dude defunct, as electro pop, R&B, and hip-hop burst their way into the pop music scene. Synthesizer and sax solos dominated, rock was at its most glam, and ravers rode the new wave all night long. It was the Thriller of an era that saw the rise of the first music videos, and everybody just wanted their MTV.

Are you a Super Freak of 80s music trivia? Can you bust out the right answers All Night Long? Well, call up your Beastie Boys (or any old Mötley Crüe) to embark on a night of Madness—then Wham!, you'll Rick-roll your way straight through this round!

BANDS 1
QUESTIONS

1 What was the name of Wham!'s debut album, released on July 9, 1983?

2 Which play by Shakespeare is also the title of a 1981 song by Dire Straits?

3 What is the real name of Culture Club's lead singer, Boy George?

4 Which Philadelphia-based pop-rock duo met for the first time while hiding from gunfire in a service elevator?

5 Which 1987 record, sharing much of its name with a US National Park, was the fifth studio album released by U2?

6 *Girls on Film*, released in 1981, was a major hit for which new-wave band?

7 The Bangles had a hit in 1987 with a cover of which Simon & Garfunkel song, which was also used on the soundtrack of the movie *Less than Zero*?

8 Which was the only Pet Shop Boys hit to reach number 1 on the Billboard Hot 100?

9 Which band consists of the duo Andy Bell and Vince Clarke, formerly a co-founder of Depeche Mode?

1 What was the name of Wham!'s debut album, released on July 9, 1983?

Fantastic

The album reached number one in the UK charts on first release, reaching triple-platinum status in the UK and gold status in the US. The Wham! duo of George Michael and Andrew Ridgeley had met at school, and were previously briefly part of a ska band called The Executive. Wham! found early success after appearing on the UK's Top of the Pops, after being a last-minute addition to the line-up after another act dropped out.

2 Which play by Shakespeare is also the title of a 1981 song by Dire Straits?

Romeo and Juliet

3 What is the real name of Culture Club's lead singer, Boy George?

George Alan O'Dowd

4 Which Philadelphia-based pop-rock duo met for the first time while hiding from gunfire in a service elevator?

Daryl Hall and John Oates

5 Which 1987 record, sharing much of its name with a US National Park, was the fifth studio album released by U2?

The Joshua Tree

6 *Girls on Film*, released in 1981, was a major hit for which new-wave band?

Duran Duran

7 The Bangles had a hit in 1987 with a cover of which Simon & Garfunkel song, which was also used on the soundtrack of the movie *Less than Zero*?

A Hazy Shade of Winter

8 Which was the only Pet Shop Boys hit to reach number 1 on the Billboard Hot 100?

West End Girls

9 Which band consists of the duo Andy Bell and Vince Clarke, formerly a co-founder of Depeche Mode?

Erasure

RAP & HIP HOP 1
QUESTIONS

1 Which three-piece group, who collaborated with Aerosmith in 1986, became the first hip hop group to have a music video broadcast on MTV?

2 What is the title of the 1989 single by Public Enemy that was created for Spike Lee's film, *Do the Right Thing*?

3 What do the initials stand for in the name of two-time Grammy winner, LL Cool J?

4 Change one letter in each word below to reveal the name of the hip hop group who recorded hit single *Can I Kick It* in 1989:

I BRIBE CALMED GUEST

5 What is the name of De La Soul's 1989 debut album, which featured the hit single *Me Myself and I*, and which was inspired by the title of a Johnny Cash song?

6 What is the alliterative two-word name of the band whose members had the nicknames "Mike D", "MCA", and "Ad-Rock"?

7 Which West-Philadelphia duo won the first Grammy Award for Best Rap Performance for their 1988 single, *Parents Just Don't Understand*?

1 Which three-piece group, who collaborated with Aerosmith in 1986, became the first hip hop group to have a music video broadcast on MTV?

Run-DMC

The trio were pioneering in other ways too, including by being the first hip hop act to appear on the cover of Rolling Stone, and the first to be nominated for a Grammy. Their collaboration with Aerosmith on the track Walk This Way led to a re-released recording, which charted higher than the original version.

2 What is the title of the 1989 single by Public Enemy that was created for Spike Lee's film, *Do the Right Thing*?

Fight the Power

3 What do the initials stand for in the name of two-time Grammy winner, LL Cool J?

"Ladies Love Cool James"

4 Change one letter in each word below to reveal the name of the hip hop group who recorded hit single *Can I Kick It* in 1989:

I BRIBE CALMED GUEST

A Tribe Called Quest

5 What is the name of De La Soul's 1989 debut album, which featured the hit single *Me Myself and I*, and which was inspired by the title of a Johnny Cash song?

3 Feet High and Rising

6 What is the alliterative two-word name of the band whose members had the nicknames "Mike D", "MCA", and "Ad-Rock"?

Beastie Boys

7 Which West-Philadelphia duo won the first Grammy Award for Best Rap Performance for their 1988 single, *Parents Just Don't Understand*?

DJ Jazzy Jeff and the Fresh Prince

POT LUCK 1
QUESTIONS

1. Which actress, famous for her starring role in the movie *Grease*, released the song *Physical* in 1981?

2. George Michael released his debut solo album in 1987. What was it called?

3. Which Grammy-Award-winning musician was responsible for the 1984 album, *Purple Rain*?

4. John Deacon, Roger Taylor, and Brian May are all members of which British rock band, formed in 1970, which continued to release a series of hits throughout the 1980s and beyond?

5. Rearrange the letters below to reveal the title of a song, originally released by Aerosmith in 1975, which became a hit again in 1986 thanks to a collaboration with hip hop group Run-DMC:

   WHY WAIL TASK (4, 4, 3)

6. Which singer, the youngest sibling of Michael Jackson, released the album *Control* in 1986?

7. *Holiday* and *Lucky Star* are both tracks from which US singer's self-titled debut album?

1 Which actress, famous for her starring role in the movie *Grease*, released the song *Physical* in 1981?

Olivia Newton-John

Physical was released as the lead single on the singer's eleventh studio album—which was also titled Physical. *The song was first offered to Rod Stewart and then Tina Turner, before finally being released by Newton-John. The single spent a record (for the 1980s) 10 weeks on the US Billboard Hot 100, in spite of being banned by several radio stations for its controversially suggestive lyrics.*

2 George Michael released his debut solo album in 1987. What was it called?

Faith

3 Which Grammy-Award-winning musician was responsible for the 1984 album, *Purple Rain*?

Prince

4 John Deacon, Roger Taylor, and Brian May are all members of which British rock band, formed in 1970, which continued to release a series of hits throughout the 1980s and beyond?

Queen

5 Rearrange the letters below to reveal the title of a song, originally released by Aerosmith in 1975, which became a hit again in 1986 thanks to a collaboration with hip hop group Run-DMC:

WHY WAIL TASK (4, 4, 3)

Walk This Way

6 Which singer, the youngest sibling of Michael Jackson, released the album *Control* in 1986?

Janet Jackson

7 *Holiday* and *Lucky Star* are both tracks from which US singer's self-titled debut album?

Madonna

LIVE AID
QUESTIONS

1 On what exact date did the original Live Aid benefit concert take place?

2 What is the title of the charity single, released seven months before the concert, which became the inspiration for the Live Aid event?

3 Which pair of musicians sang *Don't Let the Sun Go Down on Me* at the London concert, which had previously been released by one of them back in 1974?

4 Who is the only artist that appeared in both the UK and US Live Aid shows, on the same day?

5 Which singer performed the "aaaay-oh" refrain, which was later described as "the note heard round the world"?

6 What is the title of the song that Paul McCartney performed toward the end of the London show and during which his microphone failed, prompting back-up efforts from organizer Bob Geldof?

7 Restore the missing vowels, and change the spacing, to restore the name of the band who opened the concert in London with a version of *Rockin' All Over The World*:

S TT SQ

LIVE AID
ANSWERS

1 On what exact date did the original Live Aid benefit concert take place?

July 13, 1985

The fundraising concert was held simultaneously in the UK and the US, with events in both London's Wembley Stadium and the John F. Kennedy Stadium in Philadelphia. Broadcasting of the event began with the message "It's twelve noon in London, 7a.m. in Philadelphia, and around the world it's time for Live Aid".

2 What is the title of the charity single, released seven months before the concert, which became the inspiration for the Live Aid event?

Do They Know It's Christmas

3 Which pair of musicians sang *Don't Let the Sun Go Down on Me* at the London concert, which had previously been released by one of them back in 1974?

Elton John and George Michael

4 Who is the only artist that appeared in both the UK and US Live Aid shows, on the same day?

Phil Collins

5 Which singer performed the "aaaay-oh" refrain, which was later described as "the note heard round the world"?

Freddie Mercury

6 What is the title of the song that Paul McCartney performed toward the end of the London show and during which his microphone failed, prompting back-up efforts from organizer Bob Geldof?

Let It Be

7 Restore the missing vowels, and change the spacing, to restore the name of the band who opened the concert in London with a version of *Rockin' All Over The World*:

S TT SQ

Status Quo

ONE-HIT WONDERS 1
QUESTIONS

1 Which 1987 film starring Tom Cruise features the Bobby McFerrin song *Don't Worry Be Happy* as a part of its soundtrack?

2 What is the name of the Italian dance group that released *Ride on Time* in 1989, and whose video featured a lip-synching lead singer?

3 Which group recorded *Eye of the Tiger* for the film *Rocky III*, at the direct request of Sylvester Stallone?

4 Which 1982 song, originally by Dexys Midnight Runners & The Emerald Express, was later covered by the one-time band 4-4-2 as a song to support the England football team?

5 Fill in the gaps below, with one word per gap, to complete the full name of the 1989 single by Soul II Soul for which they won a Grammy Award:

Back to Life (_____ _____ _____ _____ _____)

6 Which song, covered by Barbara Gaskin and Dave Stewart in 1981, and which went to number one in the UK charts, features lyrics about a couple named Judy and Johnny?

7 What is the name of the British duo who covered *Don't Leave Me This Way*, featuring vocals from Sarah Jane Morris, which spent four weeks at the top of the UK charts?

ONE-HIT WONDERS 1
ANSWERS

1 Which 1987 film starring Tom Cruise features the Bobby McFerrin song *Don't Worry Be Happy* as a part of its soundtrack?

Cocktail

> *Although the film received largely negative reviews, its theme song went on to win two Grammys, plus a third for Bobby McFerrin's vocals. The track uses no musical instruments but instead features McFerrin creating all of the accompaniment with his voice. When the track reached number one on the Billboard Hot 100, it was the first a cappella song to achieve that feat.*

2 What is the name of the Italian dance group that released *Ride on Time* in 1989, and whose video featured a lip-synching lead singer?

Black Box

3 Which group recorded *Eye of the Tiger* for the film *Rocky III*, at the direct request of Sylvester Stallone?

Survivor

4 Which 1982 song, originally by Dexys Midnight Runners & The Emerald Express, was later covered by the one-time band 4-4-2 as a song to support the England football team?

Come On Eileen

5 Fill in the gaps below, with one word per gap, to complete the full name of the 1989 single by Soul II Soul for which they won a Grammy Award:

Back to Life (_____ _____ _____ _____ _____)

Back to Life (However Do You Want Me)

6 Which song, covered by Barbara Gaskin and Dave Stewart in 1981, and which went to number one in the UK charts, features lyrics about a couple named Judy and Johnny?

It's My Party

7 What is the name of the British duo who covered *Don't Leave Me This Way*, featuring vocals from Sarah Jane Morris, which spent four weeks at the top of the UK charts?

The Communards

ROCK & METAL
QUESTIONS

1 What is the correct styling of the name of the heavy-metal band fronted by Tommy Lee?

a. Mötley Crue
b. Mótley Crüe
c. Møtley Crü
d. Mötley Crüe

2 Which British heavy metal band, who released the album *The Number of the Beast* in 1982, is named after a supposed medieval torture device?

3 Delete one letter from each pair below to restore the name of a US thrash metal band, who released *Master of Puppets* in 1986:

MA NE TH RA XL LH IR CA AX

4 In total, how many members of US rock band Van Halen had the surname Van Halen, from 1972 through until the band's disbanding in 2020?

5 What is the title of the 1980 single by Motörhead which opens with the lyrics "If you like to gamble, I tell you I'm your man"?

6 Which Guns N' Roses song was the only one of their singles to reach number one on the Billboard Hot 100?

7 *Here I Go Again* was a hit single for which London-based band, whose singer had once been a member of Deep Purple?

ROCK & METAL
ANSWERS

1 What is the correct styling of the name of the heavy-metal band fronted by Tommy Lee?

a. Mötley Crue
b. Mótley Crüe
c. Møtley Crü
d. Mötley Crüe

d. Mötley Crüe

The addition of the dotted umlauts in the already deliberately misspelled name was supposedly inspired by the name of a German beer the band had been drinking, Löwenbräu. Known for their extravagant lifestyles and live performances, the group later came to be associated with the glam metal genre.

2 Which British heavy metal band, who released the album *The Number of the Beast* in 1982, is named after a supposed medieval torture device?

Iron Maiden

3 Delete one letter from each pair below to restore the name of a US thrash metal band, who released *Master of Puppets* in 1986:

MA NE TH RA XL LH IR CA AX

Metallica

4 In total, how many members of US rock band Van Halen had the surname Van Halen, from 1972 through until the band's disbanding in 2020?

Three

5 What is the title of the 1980 single by Motörhead which opens with the lyrics "If you like to gamble, I tell you I'm your man"?

Ace of Spades

6 Which Guns N' Roses song was the only one of their singles to reach number one on the Billboard Hot 100?

Sweet Child o' Mine

7 *Here I Go Again* was a hit single for which London-based band, whose singer had once been a member of Deep Purple?

Whitesnake

COMPLETE THE LYRICS 1
QUESTIONS

Can you fill in the missing word or words in each lyric below?

1 Dolly Parton, *9 to 5*:

"I tumble outta bed and stumble to the kitchen
Pour myself a cup of _____ "

2 Hall & Oates, *You Make My Dreams*:

"I'm down on my daydream,
Oh that _____ should be over by now"

3 Culture Club, *Karma Chameleon*:

"_____ loving in your eyes all the way
If I listen to your lies, would you say"

4 Diana Ross, *Upside Down*:

"Upside down you're turning me
You're giving love _____ "

5 Joan Jett & the Blackhearts, *I Love Rock 'n Roll*:

"I saw him standing there by the _____ machine"

6 Bonnie Tyler, *Total Eclipse of the Heart*:

"Every now and then I get a little bit _____
And you're never coming _____ "

7 Lionel Richie, *All Night Long (All Night)*:

"Well my friends the time has come
To raise the _____ and have some _____ "

COMPLETE THE LYRICS 1
ANSWERS

Can you fill in the missing word or words in each lyric below?

1 Dolly Parton, *9 to 5*:

"I tumble outta bed and stumble to the kitchen
Pour myself a cup of _____"

Ambition

> *The song was written to accompany the 1980 film of the same name in which Parton starred alongside Jane Fonda and Lily Tomlin, and later featured in a stage musical adaptation of the movie. The sound of a percussive typewriter can be heard in the song's opening bars, including the chiming of the bell heard when a new line of text begins.*

2 Hall & Oates, *You Make My Dreams*:

"I'm down on my daydream,
Oh that _____ should be over by now"

Sleepwalk

3 Culture Club, *Karma Chameleon*:

"_____ loving in your eyes all the way
If I listen to your lies, would you say"

Desert

4 Diana Ross, *Upside Down*:

"Upside down you're turning me
You're giving love _____"

Instinctively

5 Joan Jett & the Blackhearts, *I Love Rock 'n Roll*:

"I saw him standing there by the _____ machine"

Record

6 Bonnie Tyler, *Total Eclipse of the Heart*:

"Every now and then I get a little bit _____
And you're never coming _____"

Lonely; round

7 Lionel Richie, *All Night Long (All Night)*:

"Well my friends the time has come
To raise the _____ and have some _____"

Roof; fun

SOLO ARTISTS 1
QUESTIONS

1 Change one letter in each word below to reveal the name of a 1984 Grammy-Award-winning song made famous by Tina Turner:

THAT'S LONE GUT SO TO WISH AT

2 Which 1987 single by Madonna has a Spanish title, which can be translated into English as "The Beautiful Island"?

3 Who released their fourth studio album in 1989, which shared much of its name with the singer's hit single *Rhythm Nation* that also featured on the album?

4 How many studio albums did Bruce Springsteen release during the 1980s?

5 Which singer and songwriter won the Academy Award for Best Original Song with the track *Say You, Say Me*?

6 What is the name of the title track from David Bowie's fifteenth studio album, which went to number one in the UK charts and the Billboard Hot 100, and which mentions red shoes in its lyrics?

7 Which of these songs was not listed on Cyndi Lauper's debut album?

a. *Girls Just Want to Have Fun*
b. *Time After Time*
c. *True Colors*
d. *She Bop*

SOLO ARTISTS 1
ANSWERS

1 Change one letter in each word below to reveal the name of a 1984 Grammy-Award-winning song made famous by Tina Turner:

THAT'S LONE GUT SO TO WISH AT

What's Love Got to Do with It

The song won Record of the Year, Song of the Year, and Turner won the Grammy for Best Female Pop Vocal Performance. It was Turner's first Billboard Hot 100 single, and at 44 years of age, she was the oldest woman to have achieved the feat.

2 Which 1987 single by Madonna has a Spanish title, which can be translated into English as "The Beautiful Island"?

La Isla Bonita

3 Who released their fourth studio album in 1989, which shared much of its name with the singer's hit single *Rhythm Nation* that also featured on the album?

Janet Jackson

4 How many studio albums did Bruce Springsteen release during the 1980s?

Four

5 Which singer and songwriter won the Academy Award for Best Original Song with the track *Say You, Say Me*?

Lionel Richie

6 What is the name of the title track from David Bowie's fifteenth studio album, which went to number one in the UK charts and the Billboard Hot 100, and which mentions red shoes in its lyrics?

Let's Dance

7 Which of these songs was not listed on Cyndi Lauper's debut album?

a. *Girls Just Want to Have Fun*
b. *Time After Time*
c. *True Colors*
d. *She Bop*

c. *True Colors*

MOVIE SONGS 1
QUESTIONS

1 Rearrange the letters below to reveal the name of a song, featured on the *Dirty Dancing* soundtrack, that was written by the same duo who created *(I've Had) The Time of My Life*:

HUE SYNERGY (6, 4)

2 Change one letter in each word below to reveal the title of a song by Deniece Williams that featured in *Footloose*:

GET'S BEAR IN FAR SHE BOX

3 The lead singer of which band sued the creator of the *Ghostbusters* theme song, claiming it had been copied from their song *I Want a New Drug*?

4 For which film did Lionel Richie write and record the Oscar- and Grammy-Award winning song, *Say You, Say Me*?

5 Which song from *The Little Mermaid* opens with the words "The seaweed is always greener / In somebody else's lake"?

6 What is the one-word title of the 1987 film that featured the song *Nothing's Gonna Stop Us Now*, which was nominated for the Best Original Song Oscar?

7 Which German city is also the name of the group which performed *Take My Breath Away* for the 1986 film *Top Gun*, which won the Academy Award for Best Original Song?

MOVIE SONGS 1
ANSWERS

1 Rearrange the letters below to reveal the name of a song, featured on the *Dirty Dancing* soundtrack, that was written by the same duo who created *(I've Had) The Time of My Life*:

HUE SYNERGY (6, 4)

Hungry Eyes

The song enjoyed success in the US and, despite not being commercially released there, managed to break into the UK charts too. The film's soundtrack also went on to became one of the best-selling albums of all time. Hungry Eyes was recorded by Eric Carmen, who had released the hit All By Myself in the 1970s.

2 Change one letter in each word below to reveal the title of a song by Deniece Williams that featured in *Footloose*:

GET'S BEAR IN FAR SHE BOX

Let's Hear It for the Boy

3 The lead singer of which band sued the creator of the *Ghostbusters* theme song, claiming it had been copied from their song *I Want a New Drug*?

Huey Lewis and the News

4 For which film did Lionel Richie write and record the Oscar- and Grammy-Award winning song, *Say You, Say Me*?

White Nights

5 Which song from *The Little Mermaid* opens with the words "The seaweed is always greener / In somebody else's lake"?

Under the Sea

6 What is the one-word title of the 1987 film that featured the song *Nothing's Gonna Stop Us Now*, which was nominated for the Best Original Song Oscar?

Mannequin

7 Which German city is also the name of the group which performed *Take My Breath Away* for the 1986 film *Top Gun*, which won the Academy Award for Best Original Song?

Berlin

MADONNA
QUESTIONS

1 Restore the vowels, and change the spacing, to reveal the title of the film that Madonna co-starred in in 1985:

D SPRT LYSK NGS SN

2 Which US actor, who later won two Academy Awards, did Madonna marry in 1985?

3 In what year was Madonna's debut studio album, *Madonna*, first released?

4 For how many weeks did the single *Like a Virgin* stay at Number One in the Billboard Hot 100 chart?

a. 3
b. 6
c. 9
d. 12

5 With which show, a satirical take on the US movie business, did Madonna make her Broadway debut, in 1988?

6 What title did Madonna receive at the end of the 1980s from MTV, Billboard, and *Musician* magazine?

7 Which rap group opened for Madonna on her first concert tour in North America?

MADONNA
ANSWERS

1 Restore the vowels, and change the spacing, to reveal the title of the film that Madonna co-starred in in 1985:

D SPRT LYSK NGS SN

Desperately Seeking Susan

> *Also starring Rosanna Arquette, the movie centers around the two women interacting via messages that are placed in the personals section of a newspaper. It was the fifth-highest grossing movie of the year in the US, and became the then-most successful European film for its production company and distributor, Orion Pictures.*

2 Which US actor, who later won two Academy Awards, did Madonna marry in 1985?

Sean Penn

3 In what year was Madonna's debut studio album, *Madonna*, first released?

1983

4 For how many weeks did the single *Like a Virgin* stay at Number One in the Billboard Hot 100 chart?

a. 3
b. 6
c. 9
d. 12

b. 6

5 With which show, a satirical take on the US movie business, did Madonna make her Broadway debut, in 1988?

***Speed-the-Plow* at the Royale Theatre**

6 What title did Madonna receive at the end of the 1980s from MTV, Billboard, and *Musician* magazine?

Artist of the Decade

7 Which rap group opened for Madonna on her first concert tour in North America?

Beastie Boys

BANDS 2
QUESTIONS

1 Change one letter in each word below to reveal the title of a song by The Police, which won them a Grammy Award in 1980:

WON'T STANK TO CHOSE NO MY

2 What is the title of the 1985 single by Tears for Fears which opens with the line "Welcome to your life"?

3 How many sisters from the Pointer family are featured as singers on the 1982 single, *I'm So Excited*?

4 Which 1980 track by Queen, which appeared on the album *The Game*, was initially chosen as a theme song for the movie *Rocky III*, before being later replaced by *Eye of the Tiger*?

5 Which New Romantic band released their debut single *To Cut a Long Story Short* in 1980, three years before the release of hit single *True*?

6 Which two musicians make up the band Eurythmics, who scored a massive hit with *Sweet Dreams (Are Made of This)* in 1983?

7 The lead singer of which band teamed up with David Bowie in 1985 to release a cover version of *Dancing in the Street*?

1 Change one letter in each word below to reveal the title of a song by The Police, which won them a Grammy Award in 1980:

WON'T STANK TO CHOSE NO MY

Don't Stand So Close to Me

> *The song, from the band's third album* Zenyatta Mondatta, *was the best-selling single of 1980 in the UK, and won them a Grammy Award. The band then re-recorded and released the track in 1986 with a different arrangement, before splitting up later that year.*

2 What is the title of the 1985 single by Tears for Fears which opens with the line "Welcome to your life"?

Everybody Wants to Rule the World

3 How many sisters from the Pointer family are featured as singers on the 1982 single, *I'm So Excited*?

Three

4 Which 1980 track by Queen, which appeared on the album *The Game*, was initially chosen as a theme song for the movie *Rocky III*, before being later replaced by *Eye of the Tiger*?

Another One Bites the Dust

5 Which New Romantic band released their debut single *To Cut a Long Story Short* in 1980, three years before the release of hit single *True*?

Spandau Ballet

6 Which two musicians make up the band Eurythmics, who scored a massive hit with *Sweet Dreams (Are Made of This)* in 1983?

Annie Lennox and Dave Stewart

7 The lead singer of which band teamed up with David Bowie in 1985 to release a cover version of *Dancing in the Street*?

The Rolling Stones (Mick Jagger)

PRINCE
QUESTIONS

1 Rearrange the letters below to reveal the title of Prince's third studio album, released in October 1980:

TIMID N DRY (5, 4)

2 What was the name of the band Prince helped form in Minneapolis, in 1981?

3 In what year did Prince first appear on *Saturday Night Live*, singing the track *Partyup*?

4 Which hit song, released by the Bangles in 1986 but originally intended for the group Apollonia 6, did Prince write under the pseudonym of "Christopher"?

5 Which pop artist produced twelve silkscreen portraits of Prince in 1984, along with four additional works on paper?

6 Which director asked Prince to record a series of songs for a live-action adaptation of Batman?

7 Prince was asked by which iconic band to appear as the first of three opening acts during their 1981 tour?

1 Rearrange the letters below to reveal the title of Prince's third studio album, released in October 1980:

TIMID N DRY (5, 4)

Dirty Mind

Released in October 1980, the album was produced by Prince at his home studio over the course of less than two months. The album was noted for its increased punk influences, but also caused controversy over some of the topics that were covered by the various tracks on the album.

2 What was the name of the band Prince helped form in Minneapolis, in 1981?

The Time, a.k.a. Morris Day and the Time, a.k.a. The Original 7ven

3 In what year did Prince first appear on *Saturday Night Live*, singing the track *Partyup*?

1981

4 Which hit song, released by the Bangles in 1986 but originally intended for the group Apollonia 6, did Prince write under the pseudonym of "Christopher"?

Manic Monday

5 Which pop artist produced twelve silkscreen portraits of Prince in 1984, along with four additional works on paper?

Andy Warhol

6 Which director asked Prince to record a series of songs for a live-action adaptation of Batman?

Tim Burton

7 Prince was asked by which iconic band to appear as the first of three opening acts during their 1981 tour?

The Rolling Stones

WHITNEY HOUSTON
QUESTIONS

1 Change one letter in each word below to reveal Whitney Houston's first single to reach number one in both the UK and the US:

HAVING ILL BY LONE FOX YON

2 In June 1988, Whitney Houston performed at Wembley Stadium, along with other musicians, to celebrate which then-imprisoned campaigner's 70th birthday?

3 What was the title of the duet recorded by Whitney Houston with Teddy Pendergrass, a track which then appeared on her debut album?

4 On what notable day in 1985 was her debut album, *Whitney Houston*, released?

5 What was the title of Whitney Houston's somewhat unimaginatively named second album, released in 1987?

6 Whitney Houston had seven consecutive number one hits on the Billboard Hot 100 chart, beating the prior record that had been shared by which two bands?

7 Complete the title of the first single from Whitney Houston's second album by writing one word into each of the blanks below:

"I _____ _____ with _____ (_____ _____ _____)

WHITNEY HOUSTON
ANSWERS

1 Change one letter in each word below to reveal Whitney Houston's first single to reach number one in both the UK and the US:

HAVING ILL BY LONE FOX YON

Saving All My Love for You

The song had originally been recorded by Marilyn McCoo and Billy David Jr. for a 1978 album, but it had nothing like the success of the Whitney Houston version. The song stayed at number one on the Billboard Hot 100 for two weeks, and eventually certified platinum.

2 In June 1988, Whitney Houston performed at Wembley Stadium, along with other musicians, to celebrate which then-imprisoned campaigner's 70th birthday?

Nelson Mandela

3 What was the title of the duet recorded by Whitney Houston with Teddy Pendergrass, a track which then appeared on her debut album?

Hold Me

4 On what notable day in 1985 was her debut album, *Whitney Houston*, released?

Valentine's Day (14 February)

5 What was the title of Whitney Houston's somewhat unimaginatively named second album, released in 1987?

Whitney

6 Whitney Houston had seven consecutive number one hits on the Billboard Hot 100 chart, beating the prior record that had been shared by which two bands?

The Beatles and the Bee Gees, each of whom had had six consecutive number ones

7 Complete the title of the first single from Whitney Houston's second album by writing one word into each of the blanks below:

"I _____ _____ with _____
(_____ _____ _____)

I Wanna Dance with Somebody (Who Loves Me)

POT LUCK 2
QUESTIONS

1 Which 1983 duet, sung by Dolly Parton and Kenny Rogers, was written by the Bee Gees?

2 For which film was the song *Call Me* both written and performed by Blondie?

3 What is the name of INXS's only single to reach number one on the US Billboard Hot 100?

4 Which 1986 song, recorded by The Bangles, was inspired by a ferry trip during which the songwriter noticed passengers moving unsteadily in turbulent weather?

5 Which English punk rock band released *Should I Stay or Should I Go* in 1982, a track which later featured in a Levi's commercial?

6 Under what name are the married duo who released *Teardrops* listed on the song's credits?

7 Change one letter in each word below to reveal the name of a 1987 single from U2:

A SKILL RAVEN'T SOUND
WHAM A'M COOKING FUR

POT LUCK 2
ANSWERS

1 Which 1983 duet, sung by Dolly Parton and Kenny Rogers, was written by the Bee Gees?

Islands in the Stream

The single, a version of which was in fact originally written for Diana Ross, topped the charts in both the US and Australia and peaked at number seven in the UK. The chorus was notably interpolated in the later 1998 track Ghetto Supastar (That Is What You Are), *created by former Fugees member, Pras.*

2 For which film was the song *Call Me* both written and performed by Blondie?

American Gigolo

3 What is the name of INXS's only single to reach number one on the US Billboard Hot 100?

Need You Tonight

4 Which 1986 song, recorded by The Bangles, was inspired by a ferry trip during which the songwriter noticed passengers moving unsteadily in turbulent weather?

Walk Like an Egyptian

5 Which English punk rock band released *Should I Stay or Should I Go* in 1982, a track which later featured in a Levi's commercial?

The Clash

6 Under what name are the married duo who released *Teardrops* listed on the song's credits?

Womack & Womack

7 Change one letter in each word below to reveal the name of a 1987 single from U2:

A SKILL RAVEN'T SOUND WHAM A'M COOKING FUR

I Still Haven't Found What I'm Looking For

MUSIC VIDEOS
QUESTIONS

1 Which 1983 music video opens with a written assurance from Michael Jackson that the film "in no way endorses a belief in the occult"?

2 What is the title of the 1989 single by Madonna whose music video attracted condemnation from the Vatican?

3 Which household appliance is Freddie Mercury shown using at the start of the accompanying video for *I Want to Break Free*?

4 Which Australian singer released an appropriately titled 1981 single featuring a music video set in a gym?

5 Which band released *Video Killed the Radio Star*, which became the first music video to be shown on MTV?

6 What is the title of the Cyndi Lauper track whose music video opens with the singer's real-life mother cracking eggs into a bowl?

7 Replace one letter in each word below to reveal the title of the Prince song whose video opens with the singer in a bathtub:

THEN LOVES FRY

MUSIC VIDEOS
ANSWERS

1 Which 1983 music video opens with a written assurance from Michael Jackson that the film "in no way endorses a belief in the occult"?

Thriller

The short film, which functioned as the music video for Thriller, is perhaps one of the most enduring images of 1980s pop culture. In spite of its immense popularity, there is a common misconception about the film's opening sequence, in which Jackson is shown transforming into a werecat, not a wolf as is commonly assumed.

2 What is the title of the 1989 single by Madonna whose music video attracted condemnation from the Vatican?

Like a Prayer

3 Which household appliance is Freddie Mercury shown using at the start of the accompanying video for *I Want to Break Free*?

Vacuum cleaner

4 Which Australian singer released an appropriately titled 1981 single featuring a music video set in a gym?

Olivia Newton-John

5 Which band released *Video Killed the Radio Star*, which became the first music video to be shown on MTV?

The Buggles

6 What is the title of the Cyndi Lauper track whose music video opens with the singer's real-life mother cracking eggs into a bowl?

Girls Just Want to Have Fun

7 Replace one letter in each word below to reveal the title of the Prince song whose video opens with the singer in a bathtub:

THEN LOVES FRY

When Doves Cry

RAP & HIP HOP 2
QUESTIONS

1 Who released *The Message* in 1982, featuring the lyric "It's like a jungle sometimes, it makes me wonder how I keep from going under"?

2 Can you change one letter in each word to reveal the name of Ice-T's debut album, released in 1987?

THYME PASS

3 What is the title of N.W.A.'s debut album, featuring the name of a southern Los Angeles city?

4 Which all-female hip hop group released the single *Push It* in 1988?

5 For which hip hop trio was Jam Master Jay the DJ?

6 Which single, with a name that played on the title of a famous 1955 movie, was the first to be released from Public Enemy's *It Takes a Nation of Millions to Hold Us Back*?, although the album itself was actually released later than the single?

7 By what name is Stanley Kirk Burrell, who released debut album *Feel My Power* in 1987 and famously wore baggy, harem-style pants, better known?

RAP & HIP HOP 2
ANSWERS

1 Who released *The Message* in 1982, featuring the lyric "It's like a jungle sometimes, it makes me wonder how I keep from going under"?

Grandmaster Flash & The Furious Five

Although it only ever reached a peak of 62 on the US Billboard Hot 100, the song is considered to be one of the most influential hip hop tracks of all time. With its lyrical focus on social commentary—which was unusual for the genre at the time—the song has been sampled several times since its release.

2 Can you change one letter in each word to reveal the name of Ice-T's debut album, released in 1987?

THYME PASS

Rhyme Pays

3 What is the title of N.W.A.'s debut album, featuring the name of a southern Los Angeles city?

Straight Outta Compton

4 Which all-female hip hop group released the single *Push It* in 1988?

Salt-N-Pepa

5 For which hip hop trio was Jam Master Jay the DJ?

Run-DMC

6 Which single, with a name that played on the title of a famous 1955 movie, was the first to be released from Public Enemy's *It Takes a Nation of Millions to Hold Us Back?*, although the album itself was actually released later than the single?

Rebel Without a Pause

7 By what name is Stanley Kirk Burrell, who released debut album *Feel My Power* in 1987 and famously wore baggy, harem-style pants, better known?

MC Hammer

SOLO ARTISTS 2
QUESTIONS

1 Which hit song by Rick Astley won the 1988 Brit Award for Best British Single?

2 Change one letter in each word below to reveal the name of the 1981 single, released by Luther Vandross, which was previously recorded by Dionne Warwick:

I HORSE IF NUT I HOLE

3 Who released their seventeenth studio album in 1983, which was stylized as 2 ▼ 4 0 and which featured the single *I'm Still Standing*?

4 Which Australian actress and singer, known for her role in the soap *Neighbours*, had a hit with *I Should Be So Lucky* in 1987?

5 Which two artists, best known as the lead singers of the groups Earth Wind & Fire and Genesis, released *Easy Lover* in the US in 1984?

6 Which singer, known as the "Queen of Funk", featured on the single *Ain't Nobody* alongside funk band Rufus?

7 What is the title of the song recorded by Welsh musician Bonnie Tyler that appeared in the soundtrack to *Footloose* in 1984?

SOLO ARTISTS 2
ANSWERS

1 Which hit song by Rick Astley won the 1988 Brit Award for Best British Single?

Never Gonna Give You Up

> *Astley's debut single is without doubt the song he is best known for. Following the "Rickrolling" craze, which saw internet users send the video link to each other as a prank, its online video hits exceeded one billion views in 2021.*

2 Change one letter in each word below to reveal the name of the 1981 single, released by Luther Vandross, which was previously recorded by Dionne Warwick:

I HORSE IF NUT I HOLE

A House Is Not a Home

3 Who released their seventeenth studio album in 1983, which was stylized as 2 ▼ 4 0 and which featured the single *I'm Still Standing*?

Elton John—the album title was *Too Low for Zero*

4 Which Australian actress and singer, known for her role in the soap *Neighbours*, had a hit with *I Should Be So Lucky* in 1987?

Kylie Minogue

5 Which two artists, best known as the lead singers of the groups Earth Wind & Fire and Genesis, released *Easy Lover* in the US in 1984?

Philip Bailey and Phil Collins, respectively

6 Which singer, known as the "Queen of Funk", featured on the single *Ain't Nobody* alongside funk band Rufus?

Chaka Khan

7 What is the title of the song recorded by Welsh musician Bonnie Tyler that appeared in the soundtrack to *Footloose* in 1984?

Holding Out for a Hero

MICHAEL JACKSON
QUESTIONS

1 In 1980, when Michael Jackson won three American Music Awards, for which song did he win Favorite Soul/R&B Single?

2 During a performance of which song did Michael Jackson debut the moonwalk dance?

3 How many of the songs from the album *Thriller* reached the top 10 of the Billboard Hot 100?

4 Which soft-drink brand sponsored Michael Jackson throughout the 1980s?

5 In what year was Michael Jackson's sixth studio album, *Thriller*, released?

6 Which US president gave Michael Jackson an award for his keen support of alcohol and drug abuse charities, in 1984?

7 In 1988, Michael Jackson built his famous home in California, giving it what well-known name?

MICHAEL JACKSON
ANSWERS

1 In 1980, when Michael Jackson won three American Music Awards, for which song did he win Favorite Soul/R&B Single?

Don't Stop 'Til You Get Enough

Jackson won a total of 24 American Music Awards throughout his career, along with 13 Grammy Awards, 6 Brit Awards, 5 Billboard Music Awards, and literally hundreds of other awards. He also received two Emmy Award nominations, in 1983 and 1990.

2 During a performance of which song did Michael Jackson debut the moonwalk dance?

Billie Jean

3 How many of the songs from the album *Thriller* reached the top 10 of the Billboard Hot 100?

Seven

4 Which soft-drink brand sponsored Michael Jackson throughout the 1980s?

Pepsi

5 In what year was Michael Jackson's sixth studio album, *Thriller*, released?

1982

6 Which US president gave Michael Jackson an award for his keen support of alcohol and drug abuse charities, in 1984?

Ronald Reagan

7 In 1988, Michael Jackson built his famous home in California, giving it what well-known name?

Neverland Ranch

COMPLETE THE LYRICS 2
QUESTIONS

Can you fill in the missing word in each lyric below?

1 George Michael, *Faith*:

"I need some time off from that emotion
Time to pick my _____ up off the floor"

2 Whitney Houston, *How Will I Know*:

"How I will I know if he really loves me?
I say a prayer with every _____"

3 Billy Joel, *We Didn't Start the Fire*:

"We didn't start the fire
It was always _____"

4 Cyndi Lauper, *Time After Time*:

"If you fall, I will catch you
I'll be _____"

5 Toto, *Africa*:

"I hear the drums _____ tonight
But she only hears whispers"

6 Irene Cara, *Flashdance… What A Feeling*:

"What a feeling, _____ believing"

7 Madonna, *Papa Don't Preach*:

"Papa don't preach, I'm in trouble _____"

COMPLETE THE LYRICS 2
ANSWERS

Can you fill in the missing word in each lyric below?

1 George Michael, *Faith*:

"I need some time off from that emotion
Time to pick my _____ up off the floor"

Heart

> *Although initially Michael didn't intend to release the song as a single from his 1987 debut album of the same name, once he did the track went on to reach number one in the US, Canada, and Australia, peaking at number two in the UK. The opening section of the single, played on an organ, is a version of the chorus from Wham!'s previous song, Freedom.*

2 Whitney Houston, *How Will I Know*:

"How I will I know if he really loves me?
I say a prayer with every _____"

Heartbeat

3 Billy Joel, *We Didn't Start the Fire*:

"We didn't start the fire
It was always _____"

Burning

4 Cyndi Lauper, *Time After Time*:

"If you fall, I will catch you
I'll be _____"

Waiting

5 Toto, *Africa*:

"I hear the drums _____ tonight
But she only hears whispers"

Echoing

6 Irene Cara, *Flashdance... What A Feeling*:

"What a feeling,
_____ believing"

Being's

7 Madonna, *Papa Don't Preach*:

"Papa don't preach,
I'm in trouble _____"

Deep

ONE-HIT WONDERS 2
QUESTIONS

1 What is the English name of the anti-war song released by German band Nena, which was a US hit in its original German, and for which the English-language version later reached number one in the UK?

2 Which US duo with an appropriately meteorologically themed name released *It's Raining Men* in 1982?

3 Which group released *Funky Town* in 1980? Their name is a pun on the action of miming to recorded music.

4 Delete one letter from each pair below to reveal the mononym of the singer who covered *I Think We're Alone Now* in 1987:

TB OI NF FN IA NE EY

5 What is the one-word title of the song released by Toni Basil in 1982, accompanied by a music video that features the singer dancing as a cheerleader?

6 Which synthpop duo covered a version of *Tainted Love* in 1981, which had already been released twice by the original artist Gloria Jones?

7 Which song, recorded by Kim Carnes, features the name of a two-time Academy-Award-winning actress in its title?

ONE-HIT WONDERS 2
ANSWERS

1 What is the English name of the anti-war song released by German band Nena, which was a US hit in its original German, and for which the English-language version later reached number one in the UK?

99 Red Balloons

> *Released first in German, with a title of 99 Luftballons, the song peaked at number two on the US Billboard Hot 100, but failed to chart in the UK. Although the subsequent English-language version went to number one in the UK, the band later said that they disapproved of the translated lyrics, feeling that some of the original meaning had been lost.*

2 Which US duo with an appropriately meteorologically themed name released *It's Raining Men* in 1982?

The Weather Girls

3 Which group released *Funky Town* in 1980? Their name is a pun on the action of miming to recorded music.

Lipps Inc.

4 Delete one letter from each pair below to reveal the mononym of the singer who covered *I Think We're Alone Now* in 1987:

TB OI NF FN IA NE EY

Tiffany

5 What is the one-word title of the song released by Toni Basil in 1982, accompanied by a music video that features the singer dancing as a cheerleader?

Mickey

6 Which synthpop duo covered a version of *Tainted Love* in 1981, which had already been released twice by the original artist Gloria Jones?

Soft Cell

7 Which song, recorded by Kim Carnes, features the name of a two-time Academy-Award-winning actress in its title?

Bette Davis Eyes

SYNTHPOP
QUESTIONS

1 Rearrange the letters below to reveal the name of the British band created by Neil Tennant and Chris Lowe:

THEY SOB POPS (3, 4, 4)

2 Which group released *Just Can't Get Enough* in 1981, taken from their debut album *Speak & Spell*?

3 Which band released the 1983 single *Blue Monday*, whose cover art features a color code in place of words?

4 What is the title of the song that has been released three times by Norwegian band A-ha, and which was accompanied the second time by a revolutionary music video featuring pencil-sketch animation?

5 Which 1988 song by English duo Erasure was later covered by the US rock band Wheatus, and which eventually charted higher in the UK than the original?

6 What is the name of the German band who released the albums *Computer World* and *Electric Café* during the 1980s?

7 The board game *StarForce: Alpha Centauri* provided the inspiration for the name of which British band, whose lead singer is Philip Oakey?

1 Rearrange the letters below to reveal the name of the British band created by Neil Tennant and Chris Lowe:

THEY SOB POPS (3, 4, 4)

Pet Shop Boys

Before meeting his future band member in a record shop, Neil Tennant had worked as a production editor for Marvel UK, and was assistant editor of the influential music magazine, Smash Hits. The pair's West End Girls was a number one hit in both the US and the UK, was even performed at the closing ceremony to the 2012 London Olympics, and in 2020 was named the greatest UK number-one single of all time by The Guardian.

2 Which group released *Just Can't Get Enough* in 1981, taken from their debut album *Speak & Spell*?

Depeche Mode

3 Which band released the 1983 single *Blue Monday*, whose cover art features a color code in place of words?

New Order

4 What is the title of the song that has been released three times by Norwegian band A-ha, and which was accompanied the second time by a revolutionary music video featuring pencil-sketch animation?

Take On Me

5 Which 1988 song by English duo Erasure was later covered by the US rock band Wheatus, and which eventually charted higher in the UK than the original?

A Little Respect

6 What is the name of the German band who released the albums *Computer World* and *Electric Café* during the 1980s?

Kraftwerk

7 The board game *StarForce: Alpha Centauri* provided the inspiration for the name of which British band, whose lead singer is Philip Oakey?

The Human League

BANDS 3
QUESTIONS

1 Fill in the gaps below, with one letter per gap, to reveal the title of a single released by UB40 in 1983, and which had originally been recorded by Neil Diamond:

_E_ _E_ _I_E

2 Which British band released the singles *Smooth Operator* and *Your Love is King* from their 1984 album, *Diamond Life*?

3 Which Bananarama song achieved particular success in the US after being featured in the 1984 martial arts movie, *The Karate Kid*?

4 Who was the lead singer of The Smiths, who released their self-titled debut album in 1984?

5 Which Swedish pop group released the UK's biggest-selling album of 1980, which had a two-word rhyming title?

6 Delete one letter in each pair below to reveal the name of a British ska band who formed in Camden and named themselves after a Prince Buster song:

DM RA DU RN AE NS SE

7 What is the title of the 1983 debut single, which was briefly banned on UK radio, which spawned a t-shirt craze featuring part of the band's name and the song's title?

1 Fill in the gaps below, with one letter per gap, to reveal the title of a single released by UB40 in 1983, and which had originally been recorded by Neil Diamond:

_E_ _E_ _I_E

Red Red Wine

The song was originally written and recorded by Neil Diamond in 1967, and had already been covered several times before UB40 released their iconic version. The track topped the UK charts when it was originally released, and reached number one on the Billboard Hot 100 in 1988, five years later.

2 Which British band released the singles *Smooth Operator* and *Your Love is King* from their 1984 album, *Diamond Life*?

Sade

3 Which Bananarama song achieved particular success in the US after being featured in the 1984 martial arts movie, *The Karate Kid*?

Cruel Summer

4 Who was the lead singer of The Smiths, who released their self-titled debut album in 1984?

Morrissey

5 Which Swedish pop group released the UK's biggest-selling album of 1980, which had a two-word rhyming title?

ABBA, with *Super Trouper*

6 Delete one letter in each pair below to reveal the name of a British ska band who formed in Camden and named themselves after a Prince Buster song:

DM RA DU RN AE NS SE

Madness

7 What is the title of the 1983 debut single, which was briefly banned on UK radio, which spawned a t-shirt craze featuring part of the band's name and the song's title?

***Relax*—the t-shirts were printed with "Frankie Says Relax", referring to both the song and the band itself, Frankie Goes to Hollywood**

POT LUCK 3
QUESTIONS

1 Which singer released *Chain Reaction* in 1985, which had been written by the Bee Gees, and which went on to become a number one hit in the UK?

2 Which song from the album *Thriller* did Michael Jackson claim he was so absorbed in the creation of that he did not notice that his car was on fire on the highway?

3 Change one letter in each word below to reveal the title of a track by The Smiths which features the lyrics "To die by your side / Is such a heavenly way to die":

THESE IF I MIGHT WHAT NEWER GODS PUT

4 Rearrange the letters below to reveal the name of a hit song by The Stranglers which opens with a distinctive harpsichord sequence:

WRONG BLONDE (6, 5)

5 Which Wham! song, inspired by a misspelled note written by Andrew Ridgeley, became the band's first number one in the UK, repeating the feat in the US?

6 Which band released *Love Will Tear Us Apart* in 1980, a month after their lead singer's death?

7 What is the title of the 1981 single, by Australian band Men at Work, which includes a reference to the food Vegemite in its lyrics?

1 Which singer released *Chain Reaction* in 1985, which had been written by the Bee Gees, and which went on to become a number one hit in the UK?

Diana Ross

> *Written by the three Gibb brothers of the band the Bee Gees, the song features backing vocals from Barry Gibb. The song peaked at number 66 on the US Billboard Hot 100 after it was remixed and reissued, but never managed to match the success of its UK sales, where it had become Ross's second number one.*

2 Which song from the album *Thriller* did Michael Jackson claim he was so absorbed in the creation of that he did not notice that his car was on fire on the highway?

Billie Jean

3 Change one letter in each word below to reveal the title of a track by The Smiths which features the lyrics "To die by your side / Is such a heavenly way to die":

THESE IF I MIGHT WHAT NEWER GODS PUT

There Is a Light That Never Goes Out

4 Rearrange the letters below to reveal the name of a hit song by The Stranglers which opens with a distinctive harpsichord sequence:

WRONG BLONDE (6, 5)

Golden Brown

5 Which Wham! song, inspired by a misspelled note written by Andrew Ridgeley, became the band's first number one in the UK, repeating the feat in the US?

Wake Me Up Before You Go-Go

6 Which band released *Love Will Tear Us Apart* in 1980, a month after their lead singer's death?

Joy Division

7 What is the title of the 1981 single, by Australian band Men at Work, which includes a reference to the food Vegemite in its lyrics?

Down Under

MOVIE SONGS 2
QUESTIONS

1 Which 1984 album by Prince was created as the soundtrack to a concept film of the same name?

2 In which 1980 musical-theater film did singer Irene Cara star prior to co-writing and singing *Flashdance... What a Feeling* for the 1983 film, *Flashdance*?

3 In which film did the song *When the Going Gets Tough, the Tough Get Going* appear, and which had an accompanying music video featuring the film's stars, Kathleen Turner and Danny DeVito?

4 In which film, starring Dustin Hoffman, does the song *It Might Be You* appear, and which was nominated for the Academy Award for Best Original Song?

5 Change one letter in each word below to restore the name of a Modern English song which featured on the soundtrack to *Valley Girl*:

A MEET WITS YON

6 Which English new-wave band recorded *A View to a Kill*, as the title track for the 1985 James Bond film of the same name?

7 What is the title of the 1986 film starring Molly Ringwald, which features the song *If You Leave*?

MOVIE SONGS 2
ANSWERS

1 Which 1984 album by Prince was created as the soundtrack to a concept film of the same name?

Purple Rain

> *The record became Prince's first number one album in the US, and was one of the best-selling albums of the 1980s. Featuring the tracks* Let's Go Crazy, *and the titular* Purple Rain, *several of the album's songs are credited to Prince and the Revolution, who appear alongside their frontman in the film.*

2 In which 1980 musical-theater film did singer Irene Cara star prior to co-writing and singing *Flashdance... What a Feeling* for the 1983 film, *Flashdance*?

Fame

3 In which film did the song *When the Going Gets Tough, the Tough Get Going* appear, and which had an accompanying music video featuring the film's stars, Kathleen Turner and Danny DeVito?

Jewel of the Nile

4 In which film, starring Dustin Hoffman, does the song *It Might Be You* appear, and which was nominated for the Academy Award for Best Original Song?

Tootsie

5 Change one letter in each word below to restore the name of a Modern English song which featured on the soundtrack to *Valley Girl*:

A MEET WITS YON

I Melt with You

6 Which English new-wave band recorded *A View to a Kill*, as the title track for the 1985 James Bond film of the same name?

Duran Duran

7 What is the title of the 1986 film starring Molly Ringwald, which features the song *If You Leave*?

Pretty in Pink

SOLO ARTISTS 3
QUESTIONS

1. Which single by Kate Bush, released on the 1985 album of the same name, was accompanied by a music video inspired by Alfred Hitchcock's *The 39 Steps*?

2. Who released *White Wedding* in 1982, shortly after leaving the band Generation X?

3. Which song by Bryan Adams opens with the lyrics "I got my first real six string"?

4. Which 1983 single by Billy Joel was accompanied by a video showing him dressed as a mechanic, and featured his future wife Christie Brinkley?

5. Rearrange the letters below to reveal the name of George Michael's debut UK solo single:

   SLICES WERE SHARP (8, 7)

6. What is the title of the 1982 single from Paul McCartney, featuring Stevie Wonder, which addresses themes of racism?

7. Who released the album *Born in the U.S.A.* in 1984, which went on to top both the US and UK album charts?

SOLO ARTISTS 3
ANSWERS

1 Which single by Kate Bush, released on the 1985 album of the same name, was accompanied by a music video inspired by Alfred Hitchcock's *The 39 Steps*?

The Hounds of Love

Kate Bush directed the video herself, which opens with an actor mouthing the words "It's in the trees! It's coming!", and then running away from the camera. The audio is taken from the 1957 horror film, Night of the Demon, and is heard on the single before Bush begins to sing.

2 Who released *White Wedding* in 1982, shortly after leaving the band Generation X?

Billy Idol

3 Which song by Bryan Adams opens with the lyrics "I got my first real six string"?

Summer of '69

4 Which 1983 single by Billy Joel was accompanied by a video showing him dressed as a mechanic, and featured his future wife Christie Brinkley?

Uptown Girl

5 Rearrange the letters below to reveal the name of George Michael's debut UK solo single:

SLICES WERE SHARP (8, 7)

Careless Whisper

6 What is the title of the 1982 single from Paul McCartney, featuring Stevie Wonder, which addresses themes of racism?

Ebony and Ivory

7 Who released the album *Born in the U.S.A.* in 1984, which went on to top both the US and UK album charts?

Bruce Springsteen

GAMES & TECH

The 80s saw you being able to "clap on, clap off" your bedroom light, replace the boombox on your shoulder with a slick Walkman, and play games on the move—life was never the same again. The 1980s saw huge leaps in technology and greater availability, as microwaves, PCs, and VCRs started to become fixtures in the average home. It was also a golden era for video games, even though it was only the second decade in which they had existed.

Are you ready for the ultimate 80s tech trivia showdown? Don't (Alex) Kidd yourself—this round will be one for the ages—so get your Game (Boy) on, boot up your brain's OS, and set out on the ultimate (Police, King's or Hero's) Quest to finally answer one of life's greatest unsolved mysteries: Where in the World is Carmen Sandiago?

DONKEY KONG
QUESTIONS

1. In the original 1981 *Donkey Kong* arcade game, the main character was originally named Jumpman. What was he later renamed to, thereby marking the first appearance of a popular video-game character?

2. For what system was *Donkey Kong II* released, in 1983?

3. Who is the villain in 1982's *Donkey Kong Jr.*?

4. On the final screen of each level of *Donkey Kong*, how does the main character defeat Donkey Kong?

5. In the 1983 game, *Donkey Kong 3*, the player controls a character named Stanley. What is Stanley's job?

6. Who is Donkey Kong tasked with rescuing, in the original game of the same name?

7. As well as chains and ropes, what other things can DK Jr. grab and climb in *Donkey Kong Jr.*?

DONKEY KONG
ANSWERS

1 In the original 1981 *Donkey Kong* arcade game, the main character was originally named Jumpman. What was he later renamed to, therefore marking the first appearance of a popular video-game character?

Donkey Kong

> Donkey Kong *was originally a game in which an unnamed character had to escape a maze, at which point he did not yet have a jumping ability. This was later changed as his creator, Shigeru Miyamoto, mused that "if you had a barrel rolling toward you, what would you do?". The name Jumpman therefore followed naturally from this development step.*

2 For what system was *Donkey Kong II* released, in 1983?

Game & Watch Vertical Multi Screen

3 Who is the villain in 1982's *Donkey Kong Jr.?*

Mario

4 On the final screen of each level of *Donkey Kong*, how does the main character defeat Donkey Kong?

He must remove all the yellow steel segments by walking or jumping over them

5 In the 1983 game, *Donkey Kong 3*, the player controls a character named Stanley. What is Stanley's job?

Bug exterminator

6 Who is Donkey Kong tasked with rescuing, in the original game of the same name?

Pauline

7 As well as chains and ropes, what other things can DK Jr. grab and climb in *Donkey Kong Jr.?*

Vines

HOME CONSOLES 1
QUESTIONS

1 *E.T. the Extra-Terrestrial* was a 1982 game released for which best-selling console?

2 By what name was a revised version of the *Sega Mark III* console better known by in the West?

3 Which console was the first to offer a home version of Nintendo's arcade hit, *Donkey Kong*?

4 The Atari 7800, released in 1986 and the first Atari console that they did not design themselves, was sold with which arcade racing sequel as a pack-in game?

5 Nintendo sold a robot-like accessory for its *NES* console, known as R.O.B. —but what did these initials stand for?

6 As well as a directional pad and A and B buttons, what two other buttons appeared on the front side of the Game Boy?

7 The Atari 5200 console contained almost exactly the same hardware as which two similar Atari 8-bit home computers?

1 *E.T. the Extra-Terrestrial* was a 1982 game released for which best-selling console?

Atari 2600 / Atari VCS

> Atari thought the game would be a huge success, so manufactured vast quantities of the cartridge. Each cartridge required its own circuit board and microchips so was expensive to make, but unfortunately the game was rushed to market and widely criticized for its terrible gameplay and graphics. Its subsequent failure led to enormous losses for Atari, and eventually many unsold copies of the game were buried in the New Mexico desert and then covered in concrete.

2 By what name was a revised version of the *Sega Mark III* console better known by in the West?

Sega Master System

3 Which console was the first to offer a home version of Nintendo's arcade hit, *Donkey Kong*?

ColecoVision

4 The Atari 7800, released in 1986 and the first Atari console that they did not design themselves, was sold with which arcade racing sequel as a pack-in game?

Pole Position II

5 Nintendo sold a robot-like accessory for its *NES* console, known as R.O.B.—but what did these initials stand for?

Robotic Operating Buddy

6 As well as a directional pad and A and B buttons, what two other buttons appeared on the front side of the Game Boy?

START and SELECT

7 The Atari 5200 console contained almost exactly the same hardware as which two similar Atari 8-bit home computers?

Atari 400 / Atari 800

TETRIS
QUESTIONS

1 According to the instructions for the Game Boy version of *Tetris*, what name is given to the achievement of simultaneously removing four lines at once?

2 From which country did *Tetris* originate?

3 How many different types of tetromino are there in *Tetris*?

4 In what year was the first commercial version of *Tetris* released outside its original country, originally for the PC?

5 The name "*Tetris*" comes from a combination of "tetra", meaning "four", and which popular sport?

6 How many blocks wide is the field in 1989's Game Boy video game *Tetris*?

7 The first name of the original developer of *Tetris* is Alexey, but what is his surname?

1 According to the instructions for the Game Boy version of *Tetris*, what name is given to the achievement of simultaneously removing four lines at once?

A "Tetris"

In a somewhat uninspired naming strategy, completing two lines at once is referred to as a "double", and three lines at once as a "triple". The Game Boy version was more innovative, however, in introducing a two-player version in which two Game Boys could be linked via a cable for a real-time battle. Each time a player completed a double, triple, or Tetris they would send one, two or four lines respectively to their opponent's grid.

2 From which country did *Tetris* originate?

The USSR / Soviet Union

3 How many different types of tetromino are there in *Tetris*?

Seven

4 In what year was the first commercial version of *Tetris* released outside its original country, originally for the PC?

1987

5 The name "*Tetris*" comes from a combination of "tetra", meaning "four", and which popular sport?

Tennis

6 How many blocks wide is the field in 1989's Game Boy video game *Tetris*?

10

7 The first name of the original developer of *Tetris* is Alexey, but what is his surname?

Pajitnov

HOME COMPUTERS
QUESTIONS

1 Which 1980s machine is the bestselling single home computer of all time?

2 Apple released their first computer that was marketed as "portable" in 1984. What was its name?

3 What do the letters "CPC" stand for in the title of the personal computer, Amstrad CPC?

4 Atari released their first 16-bit home computers in 1985, under what general name?

5 What was the name of the successor to Sinclair's breakthrough home computer, the ZX80?

6 In what year was the first ever IBM PC released, becoming the basis for de facto standard that followed?

7 The Apple Macintosh was the first successful home computer with a modern desktop interface. In what year was it originally released?

1 Which 1980s machine is the bestselling single home computer of all time?

Commodore 64

With sales estimates of around 12.5 million units, the Commodore 64—named after its 64 kilobytes of memory—was one of the more powerful home computers for its time. It was also one of the first computers to achieve widespread sale in retail stores, rather than just specialist computer stores, and was keenly priced for the time.

2 Apple released their first computer that was marketed as "portable" in 1984. What was its name?

Apple IIc

3 What do the letters "CPC" stand for in the title of the personal computer, Amstrad CPC?

Color Personal Computer

4 Atari released their first 16-bit home computers in 1985, under what general name?

Atari ST

5 What was the name of the successor to Sinclair's breakthrough home computer, the ZX80?

ZX81

6 In what year was the first ever IBM PC released, becoming the basis for de facto standard that followed?

1981

7 The Apple Macintosh was the first successful home computer with a modern desktop interface. In what year was it originally released?

1984

ZELDA
QUESTIONS

1. In which fantasy kingdom are the adventures in *The Legend of Zelda* set?

2. Who is the main antagonist in *The Legend of Zelda*, as well as most of the franchise?

3. How many pieces has the Triforce of Wisdom been split into, in the original *The Legend of Zelda*?

4. In the original Japanese release of the first Zelda game, what additional system hardware was required? It was no longer a requirement by the time it was later released in the West.

5. What change in game style was notable when progressing from the original game to 1987's *Zelda II: The Adventure of Link*?

6. In their original releases, what was special about the color of the original two Zelda games's cartridges?

7. In *Zelda II: The Adventure of Link*, what does Link gain that he can use to upgrade his magic and attack powers?

1 In which fantasy kingdom are the adventures in *The Legend of Zelda* set?

Hyrule

The co-creator of Zelda, Shigeru Miyamoto, described Hyrule as "a miniature garden that you can put into a drawer and revisit anytime you like", basing it on his childhood memories of the Kyoto countryside—but populated with monsters to avoid or battle, and complex dungeons to explore and solve puzzles in.

2 Who is the main antagonist in *The Legend of Zelda*, as well as most of the franchise?

Ganon

3 How many pieces has the Triforce of Wisdom been split into, in the original *The Legend of Zelda*?

8

4 In the original Japanese release of the first Zelda game, what additional system hardware was required? It was no longer a requirement by the time it was later released in the West.

The Famicom Disk System—it was later adapted to run from a normal cartridge

5 What change in game style was notable when progressing from the original game to 1987's *Zelda II: The Adventure of Link*?

A switch from top-down to side-scrolling gaming

6 In their original releases, what was special about the color of the original two Zelda games's cartridges?

They were gold-colored, instead of gray

7 In *Zelda II: The Adventure of Link*, what does Link gain that he can use to upgrade his magic and attack powers?

Experience points

FROGGER
QUESTIONS

1. Which video game company developed the original *Frogger* game?

2. Once a frog died, what symbol was used to show the location of their death?

3. How many "frog homes" are there at the top of the screen in a game of *Frogger*?

4. How many seconds do you have to guide a frog to one of the frog homes?

5. How many points do you gain with every forward step in *Frogger*?

6. The *Frogger* game screen is divided into two halves, featuring a road and which other main hazard?

7. Which two different creatures sometimes appear in the frog homes, other than the frogs themselves?

1 Which video game company developed the original *Frogger* game?

Konami

In 1981, Frogger became one of the top-grossing arcade games in North America. It was such a cultural icon that it later featured in an episode of Seinfeld, in which George Costanza tries to cross a busy road—as the frog must do in-game—while pushing an actual Frogger arcade machine.

2 Once a frog died, what symbol was used to show the location of their death?

Skull and crossbones

3 How many "frog homes" are there at the top of the screen in a game of *Frogger*?

Five

4 How many seconds do you have to guide a frog to one of the frog homes?

Thirty

5 How many points do you gain with every forward step in *Frogger*?

10 points

6 The *Frogger* game screen is divided into two halves, featuring a road and which other main hazard?

A river

7 Which two different creatures sometimes appear in the frog homes, other than the frogs themselves?

Insects and alligators

80s GAMES & TECH

INTERACTIVE TOYS
QUESTIONS

1 What was the name of Nintendo's very first handheld electronic gaming system?

2 Texas Instruments introduced the Speak & Spell in 1978, but which two follow-up products in the series did they release in 1980?

3 What Hasbro Playskool product, which lit up when squeezed, was marketed with the line "They're all your goodnight friends"?

4 Tom Hanks's and Robert Loggia's characters play the tune "Chopsticks" on what toy-store item in the 1988 movie, *Big*?

5 What was the name of the cuddly, talking, bear-like creature that was the bestselling toy of 1985 and 1986?

6 In an attempt to fight back against the rising dominance of video games, which model train and car manufacturer created the *3DS* space system, in which track pieces could be fastened to walls and the player must shoot the physically moving target that travels along them?

7 What was the name of the digital Etch A Sketch product, released in 1986, that let you store up to twelve frames of pictures and then assemble them into a moving sequence?

1 What was the name of Nintendo's very first handheld electronic gaming system?

Game & Watch

> *The product was inspired after its creator, Gunpei Yokoi, watched a bored businessman playing with his LCD calculator on a train by pressing the buttons in various ways. It was an immediate success, and led to the development of the modern "d-pad" used to control player motion on many subsequent game controllers. Ultimately, 61 different varieties of Game & Watch were released.*

2 Texas Instruments introduced the Speak & Spell in 1978, but which two follow-up products in the series did they release in 1980?

Speak & Read and Speak & Math

3 What Hasbro Playskool product, which lit up when squeezed, was marketed with the line "They're all your goodnight friends"?

Glo Worm

4 Tom Hanks's and Robert Loggia's characters play the tune "Chopsticks" on what toy-store item in the 1988 movie, *Big*?

A giant piano dance mat

5 What was the name of the cuddly, talking, bear-like creature that was the bestselling toy of 1985 and 1986?

Teddy Ruxpin

6 In an attempt to fight back against the rising dominance of video games, which model train and car manufacturer created the *3DS* space system, in which track pieces could be fastened to walls and the player must shoot the physically moving target that travels along them?

Hornby

7 What was the name of the digital Etch A Sketch product, released in 1986, that let you store up to twelve frames of pictures and then assemble them into a moving sequence?

Etch A Sketch Animator

POT LUCK
QUESTIONS

1 What is the profession of Samus Aran in the popular *Metroid* series of video games?

2 Which massively successful 1986 Sega arcade driving game allowed the player to choose which road to follow at the end of each stage, leading to five possible final destinations?

3 Disney animator Don Bluth oversaw the animated content for which 1983 game, famous for its movie-quality animations that played straight from LaserDisc?

4 What was the North American game of the Olympic-themed sports game known as *Hyper Olympic* in most other territories?

5 In which 1980 Atari arcade game did players use a trackball to launch weapons that would defend six cities from a series of incoming enemy attacks?

6 Which company released *Robotron: 2084* into arcades in 1982?

7 What was notable about the graphical style used in the 1982 arcade game, *Q*bert*?

1. What is the profession of Samus Aran in the popular *Metroid* series of video games?

Bounty hunter

> *First released for the NES in 1986, the game was unusual for its time for featuring a female protagonist, although this was primarily a story-only element since she wears a spacesuit with helmet throughout the game. Focused on multi-screen exploration, the game was so influential it gave its name to its genre – which is now known as "Metroidvania". It was five years before the first sequel appeared, but there are now many games in the series.*

2. Which massively successful 1986 Sega arcade driving game allowed the player to choose which road to follow at the end of each stage, leading to five possible final destinations?

Out Run

3. Disney animator Don Bluth oversaw the animated content for which 1983 game, famous for its movie-quality animations that played straight from LaserDisc?

Dragon's Lair

4. What was the North American game of the Olympic-themed sports game known as *Hyper Olympic* in most other territories?

Track & Field

5. In which 1980 Atari arcade game did players use a trackball to launch weapons that would defend six cities from a series of incoming enemy attacks?

Missile Command

6. Which company released *Robotron: 2084* into arcades in 1982?

Williams Electronics

7. What was notable about the graphical style used in the 1982 arcade game, *Q*bert*?

It used 2D isometric graphics to create a 3D effect

PAC-MAN
QUESTIONS

1 What are the four flashing dots that are found in the *Pac-Man* maze known as?

2 What is the nickname of the orange ghost in the original *Pac-Man* game?

3 Which company released the original Japanese arcade version of *Pac-Man*?

4 What was the name of the very first *Pac-Man* sequel created by the original developers?

5 After the initial cherry, which fruit appears next for Pac-Man to eat?

6 The different colors of ghosts have different personalities, but which color ghost most directly chases Pac-Man?

7 At what level does the original arcade *Pac-Man* become unplayable, due to a bug?

8 What 1982 *Pac-Man* sequel began development under the title *Crazy Otto*?

9 How many dots must Pac-Man eat to clear each maze?
a. 166 dots
b. 202 dots
c. 244 dots
d. 288 dots

1 What are the four flashing dots that are found in the *Pac-Man* maze known as?

Power Pellets (also known as Energizers)

> The original Japanese title for Pac-Man was Puckman, but the name was changed for Midway's North American release in order to avoid a tempting vandalization of the arcade cabinet's name that might otherwise easily take place. The game was originally partially named due to the main character's visual similarity to a hockey puck.

2 What is the nickname of the orange ghost in the original *Pac-Man* game?

Clyde—and the character is named Pokey

3 Which company released the original Japanese arcade version of *Pac-Man*?

Namco

4 What was the name of the very first *Pac-Man* sequel created by the original developers?

Super Pac-Man

5 After the initial cherry, which fruit appears next for Pac-Man to eat?

Strawberry

6 The different colors of ghosts have different personalities, but which color ghost most directly chases Pac-Man?

Red

7 At what level does the original arcade *Pac-Man* become unplayable, due to a bug?

256

8 What 1982 *Pac-Man* sequel began development under the title *Crazy Otto*?

Ms. Pac-Man

9 How many dots must Pac-Man eat to clear each maze?

a. 166 dots
b. 202 dots
c. 244 dots
d. 288 dots

c. 244 dots

HOME CONSOLES 2
QUESTIONS

1 By what name was the *Nintendo Entertainment System* (*NES*) known in Japan?

2 By what name was the *PC Engine* console known in North America?

3 Which Japanese company released the *SG-1000* console, in 1983?

4 What was the name of the home console standard, which only achieved modest success outside Japan, created by both Microsoft and ASCII Corporation and that was announced in 1983?

5 In what year was the first installment of the *Final Fantasy* series, originally available only in Japanese, released for the *NES*?

6 Which was the first mainstream console game to use battery backup to maintain save files between sessions?

7 Known as Bowser in later games, what name is given to the antagonist in 1985's *Super Mario Bros.*?

HOME CONSOLES 2
ANSWERS

1 By what name was the *Nintendo Entertainment System* (*NES*) known in Japan?

Famicom / Family Computer

The system's Japanese name suggests a device that could also be used as a general-purpose machine for all the family, but for the North American release, more than two years later than the original Japanese release, the name was changed to more accurately represent the device's target market. The bold red and white color scheme of the Japanese version was also changed to a muted gray for other markets.

2 By what name was the *PC Engine* console known in North America?

TurboGrafx-16

3 Which Japanese company released the *SG-1000* console, in 1983?

Sega

4 What was the name of the home console standard, which only achieved modest success outside Japan, created by both Microsoft and ASCII Corporation and that was announced in 1983?

MSX

5 In what year was the first installment of the *Final Fantasy* series, originally available only in Japanese, released for the *NES*?

1987

6 Which was the first mainstream console game to use battery backup to maintain save files between sessions?

The Legend of Zelda

7 Known as Bowser in later games, what name is given to the antagonist in 1985's *Super Mario Bros.*?

King Koopa